# Life in the Vine

**The Biblical Mandate of Spiritual Fruitfulness**

**The Biblical Mandate of Spiritual Fruitfulness**

# Roger W. F. Skepple

EDEN BOOK PRESS • MORROW GEORGIA

EDEN BOOK PRESS
Morrow, Georgia, USA

Unless otherwise noted, Scripture taken are from the *New American Standard Bible*, © 1960, 1962, 1963, 1968, 1871, 1972, 1973, 1975, 1977, by The Lockman Foundation. Used by permission.

ISBN 978-0966056266
Suggested Subject Headings: Theology, Doctrinal Studies, Christian Living, Salvation, Soteriology, Discipleship, Spiritual Growth

**Life in the Vine**
© 2017 Roger W. F. Skepple. All rights reserved. Printed in the United States of America.

Cover Designer: Joseph E. Banks

No part of this book may be reproduced without written permission, except for brief quotations in books and critical reviews.

*Thank you . . .*

*to the many believers over the years
who have allowed me to communicate
the truth of God to them and who have embraced
the mandate of fruitfulness.*

*to Ken Simmons, a dear friend and a fellow elder
at Berean Bible Baptist Church,
for reading the manuscript.*

*to Rachel Robinson, a dear friend and student
of the Word of God, for reading the manuscript
and offering invaluable suggestions
into ways to increase its impact on believers' lives.*

*to Teresa Skepple, my wife and best friend,
for your support, encouragement,
and challenging me to take the time to encourage
others through God's Word.*

# Contents

| | | |
|---|---|---|
| Preface | | 9 |
| Introduction | | 11 |
| 1. | The Context of the Parable | 17 |
| 2. | The Metaphor of the Vine | 29 |
| 3. | The Role of the Father and Son in Your Fruitfulness | 43 |
| 4. | The Fact of Fruitlessness in the Church | 57 |
| 5. | The Fact of Fruitfulness in the Church | 67 |
| 6. | Biblical Sketches of Spiritual Fruitfulness | 77 |
| 7. | The Prerequisite of Fruitfulness | 89 |

| 8. | The Roadmap to Fruitfulness | 99 |
|---|---|---|
| 9. | The Judas Branch:<br>The Reason for Fruitlessness | 111 |
| 10. | The Judas Branch:<br>The Reaction to Fruitlessness and Its Result | 119 |
| 11. | The Fertilizer of Fruitfulness:<br>Obedience to the Word | 127 |
| 12. | The Fertilizer of Fruitfulness:<br>Glorifying God and Loving Christ | 135 |

| Conclusion | 145 |
|---|---|
| Appendix A: A Life Devoid of the Spirit's Control | 147 |
| Appendix B: A Life Manifesting the Spirit's Control | 159 |
| Notes | 175 |

# Preface

If you have spent any length of time within Christian circles, as I have, you are aware of the fact that there exists various points of view on the Christian life, in a practical sense. The viewpoints of the Christian life I experienced in childhood differed from that which I experienced in my late teens, which differed again from what I experienced in my young adult life. Some of you may be able to empathize with me in this matter. Everything from what has been termed the "higher life" all the way to the idea of the "carnal Christian" finds a place within the context of the Christian church.

Higher life adherents advocate for a higher plane of the Christian experience than the transformation that takes place through the sinner's encounter with the gospel at conversion. Such a plane is attained by yielding oneself in increasing fashion to the working of the Holy Spirit. Such a yielding ultimately leads to another work of grace or "second work" of grace distinct from conversion. This second work, the second blessing, leads to a higher Christian life in which advocates hold that ongoing earthly sin is either greatly reduced or even completely eradicated. Such an experience may be referred to as "entire sanctification".

The carnal Christian takes a place at the opposite end of the spectrum from the advocates of the higher life perspective. Although the Bible does refer to a group of believers as "carnal" in 1 Corinthians 3:1-3, adherents to the carnal Christian point of view believe that the sinfulness of the believer which results in them being labeled as carnal is not a manifestation of immaturity, but of constant and persistent resistence to the working of the Holy Spirit in their lives. Because of this, there are three distinct possible types of spiritual life possessed by those who are converted: baby Christians (immature), Christians (mature/maturing), and carnal Christians (fleshly). In this perspective the carnal Christian lives, not by the fruit of the Spirit, but by the works of the flesh, and may in fact do so for all or the majority of his earthly Christian life.

The purpose of *Life in the Vine* is not to directly refute these positions or the other multiple positions between these two ends of the spectrum of belief about the spiritual life, but rather to present an alternative understanding of the Christian life overall. As such, the goal of this book is to layout one key aspect to the Christian life described as spiritual fruitfulness. This is not spiritual fruitfulness for a few who can attain it or as an optional way of approaching the Christian life that will also result in one arriving in heaven at the end of their life. Rather, *Life in the Vine* contends that spiritual fruitfulness is accomplished in every person who experiences the true regenerating work of the Lord God Himself that coincides with conversion. This mandate of spiritual fruitfulness was Jesus' exact point in the parable of the vine proclaimed in John 15.

# Introduction

## Life in the Vine
## The Biblical Prototype of the Christian Life

*And the one on whom seed was sown on the good soil,
this is the man who hears the word and understands it;
who indeed bears fruit, and brings forth,
some a hundredfold, some sixty, and some thirty.
Matthew 13:23*

Almost thirty years ago, while a student studying for the ministry, I wrote a term paper that would come to revolutionize not only my own Christian experience, but would come to impact both the tone and the content of my instruction from that point on. In fact, I am still learning implications from the biblical truths discovered from that study many years ago. It was a study of John 15:1-11 and the subject was what I came to call the apostatical warnings of the New Testament, that is, the warnings against apostasy within the teaching of the New Testament. The essence of what I argued in that paper was that the warnings regarding apostasy within the New Testament epistles, directed towards those within the church, find their foundation or epicenter in the teachings of Jesus contained in John 15. The core of Jesus' teaching found in this chapter is that the true believer brings forth spiritual fruit, while the false believer does not. In other words, the mandate of spiritual fruitfulness.

But the matter of bearing fruit in the believer's life is not just to supply the foundation for understanding the manifestation of the negative reality of apostasy and its existence in the local church. Fruitfulness is much more than that. Ultimately the Bible's concern with fruitfulness in the Christian experience is because it expresses Christianity in such positive terms.

Consider the concept of fruit. What does the image of fruit communicate? One aspect of fruit that no doubt comes to mind is that fruit is the natural outgrowth of something. In other words, when all the substances necessary for growth are in place, fruit will naturally and spontaneously come forth. There is no need to force an apple tree to produce apples. Is there sunshine, rain, and good soil? If there is, then apples appear, plain and simple. So too, has a person truly been born again, are they truly indwelt by Jesus Christ, through the Holy Spirit? If so, they are going to bear fruit. Fruit is a natural consequence of the preconditions to growth. Is it any surprise that the "children of the light" would produce "the fruit of the light" (Eph. 5:6-9)?

The idea of fruit has even further implications. There is with fruit an organic connection between the fruit and that which produces the fruit. Someone would be shocked indeed to come upon an orange tree bearing figs or a grape vine producing watermelons. When one examines the fruit of a plant it bears a genome connection with the plant that bore it. So, is it surprising that Ephesians refers to the fruit of the believer's life as the "fruit of light," given the fact that believers are "children of light" (5:8), born of the "Father of lights" (Jam. 1:17-18)? Since the light is the light of God Himself, thus the fruit will have a direct relationship to the character and nature of God, the source of that light. This cannot but be the case since the fruit is of the light.

However, there is still more to the concept of fruit. There are no two pieces of fruit that are exactly the same. Now they are exactly the same in that all the fruit on an apple tree are apples. So there is sameness on the genome level, as already noted. But, as one examines the individual apples on that tree, it becomes clear that they are not all the same on the appearance level. Each apple, although it clearly and obviously is an apple, also bears some unique characteristics to its fruitiness. There is diversity within the God given sameness of fruits on trees. Such a reality is the evidence of the hand of God. So, too, fruit appears in different strengths and amounts between believers (Mt. 13:23).

Consider this as related to the previous point, fruit also manifests itself in degrees. A tree does not bring forth its fruit immediately, but rather it bears its fruit in degrees. I remember when my father planted our first grapevine in our backyard. For the first two or three summers it only brought forth leaves. Its growth was steady, but I wondered if we would ever actually see grapes hanging from its thin branches. It made its way across the lattice that my father had constructed, spreading its branches like thin arms, showing many leaves, but still no fruit. Then in the third or fourth year of its steady growth some blooms appeared in many different places along its now hardy branches, which was the preliminary fruit, not yet edible.

It was only after this stage, a summer or two later, that these blooms turned to bunches of grapes that we could actually harvest for juicy grapes. Each summer after that point, until my father got rid of the vine, it produced more and more fruit. Fruit is of such a nature that it is produced through development and in degrees. It is not instantaneous, but the plant's growth towards fruitfulness and its growth throughout its fruitfulness is nonetheless steady and sure. The growth of fruit in the believer's life might seem to be quick at first, sprouting leaves and foliage, but the true fruit will come by progressive, steady maturation. But even with that, the maturation will not cease, but it will bear more fruit and much fruit for the Savior, who brings it forth. The Scriptures use the illustration of human growth in this very same fashion to communicate growth through progress and degrees, from childhood, to young adulthood, to fully mature adulthood (cf. 1 Jn. 2:12-14).

Think about one final aspect of fruit. It cannot be mass produced by human methods or systems. Rather, it springs forth from within the fruit-bearing being. There is something within pineapple trees that forces the fruit forth. Given the proper divinely created preconditions, if the pineapple tree is not to bear fruit, you must force it not to bear fruit by chopping it down. There is something within the pineapple, coconut, soursop, apple, or any other type of tree that compels the production of fruit. The fruit, in a real sense, comes from

## INTRODUCTION

within the plant and necessarily does so. This may be referred to as the principle of life, the fruit's life, that exists within the plant itself. John 15 goes a long way in explaining this final fact and stands as the basis of the necessity of bearing fruit for the true believer.

# 1
# The Context of the Parable

*Jesus, knowing that the Father had given*
*all things into His hands, and that He had come*
*forth from God, and was going back to God,*
*rose from supper, and laid aside His garments;*
*and taking a towel, He girded Himself about.*
*John 13:3-4*

As stated in the introduction, I still remember the day my father brought home the very first grapevine I had ever seen in person. It didn't look like much, but he reassured us all that we would eventually have our very own grapes. Of course, as a lover of grapes, like most of us, this sounded good to me. My father, although an educator, was also a man of the outdoors and spent copious amounts of time working in and on the yard and the garden that he and my mother kept. I think this was because, although Canadians, they were born and raised in Antigua, W.I.

Well, to my chagrin, no grapes appeared after the first year and even after the second year. To me it seemed like a fruitless project. The vine's lack of fruit did not deter my father who kept at the fertilizing and pruning anyway. Surely this was a waste of time, or so I thought, until the third or fourth year, and finally the sight of fruit. My father understood grapevines, while I did not. To the vine, my father was the vinedresser, and it is this agricultural background that provides the context for the parable of the vine in John 15.

The fifteenth chapter of John's gospel is part of what is known as the Upper Room Discourse and is probably on par, fame wise, with the Sermon on the Mount. Although similar in that they were both communicated to the disciples (cf. Mt. 5:1-2 and Jn. 13:1-3), both of these extended teaching sequences of Christ contain some pretty stark differences. For example, the sermon was unidirectional, Jesus speaking to the disciples, while the discourse was interactive throughout much of its communication. Key throughout the sermon was the concept of personal righteousness, what it was and from where it truly originated, while the relationships of the believer stood out strongly in the discourse.

Of course, there are many more differences that exist between these two divisions of their respective gospels, which can be summarized around the fact that they were given at two very different times in the ministry of Jesus. The sermon came right at the beginning of Jesus' public ministry, even before all of the twelve disciples had been selected, while the discourse occurred at the end of His three years with them. So, in the sermon Jesus was introducing His concerns to these men, concerns that would drive His three-year relationship with them. On the other hand, in the discourse, Jesus was pressing home His teachings and concerns for them as He prepared to leave them.

The timing of the discourse is one of the most important pieces of information that one must recognize to grasp the importance of this major teaching time of Christ. This was a farewell speech. We can see from this fact just how critical these final words and the subjects with which they dealt would have been to the Lord and for the disciples. Given the timing of these words, Jesus would have communicated the very heart of His instruction, the core of the new teaching He had introduced to them over the previous three years.

Thus, although the disciples did not fully grasp this fact and its implications until after His death and resurrection, it was nonetheless meant to galvanize the teaching ministry of Jesus into its major themes and ideas for them. An overview of the content of this discourse exposes the critical subjects engaged by Jesus Christ, subjects that will ultimately set up the climax of the entire discourse, which was His prayer for the disciples recorded in John 17.

The discourse began, interestingly enough, not with words from the Savior, but with the actions of the Savior.

*The Primacy of Loving Humility*

This entire moment in the life of Christ was set within the context of an unbelievable act on the part of the Savior, the washing of the disciples' feet. The actions of Christ, and John's decision to record them before he presented the discourse itself, were meant to communicate to the reader the weightiness of what was taking place and the decisive manner in which Jesus was carrying it out.

Clearly, what was meant to be communicated was that Jesus did this not out of confusion over who He was. He did it not because He misunderstood His nature and character. It was not failure to comprehend that drove Him to do it. Rather, Jesus did it because He knew who He was and wanted to communicate a reality that would be etched into the minds and consciousness of the disciples forever. The structuring of John's introduction bore this fact out. John wrote,

> Now before the Feast of the Passover, Jesus knowing that His hour had come that He should depart out of this world to the Father, having loved His own who were in the world, He loved them to the end. And during supper, the devil having already put into the heart of Judas Iscariot, the son of Simon, to betray Him, Jesus, knowing that the Father had given all things into His hands, and that He had come forth from God, and was going back to God, rose from supper, and laid aside His garments; and taking a towel, He girded Himself about (13:1-4).

John's framing of this event communicated the conscious and deliberate manner in which Jesus would carry out the act of washing the disciples' feet, which followed.

The key marker in John's structure was that although the subject, Jesus, was introduced in verse one, it would not be until

## THE CONTEXT OF THE PARABLE

verse four, that John would actually indicate what Jesus began to do. John had clearly come to realize that this was to set up the immediate actions of Christ as a climactic event taking place in the very beginning of the discourse. As such, he set up the reader to understand this.

John opened the new division in this manner, "Now before the Feast of the Passover, Jesus." With these words, John introduced the time of the following events, "before the Feast of the Passover," as well as the subject of his statement, "Jesus." However, the verbal idea of what Jesus did would not occur until John wrote in 13:4, "rose from supper, and laid aside His garments; and taking a towel, He girded Himself about."

One is left to conclude, then, that the rest of 13:1 to 13:3 were simply intended to describe Jesus, telling the reader a couple of important realities that establish the weightiness of Jesus' actions. John communicated what Jesus knew, that is, what He was aware of, when He performed this act, as well as what had occurred before the action took place.

First, John identified the knowledge that Jesus possessed in 13:1-3. His knowledge encompassed the time, in that it was time for his departure, as well as the fulness of His divine position, in that He was the vice-regent of God Himself. These might be understood as subplots. Jesus was leaving, having successfully accomplished His Father's will. He loved His own and He did so until the end, He was going to take His throne, and He was headed back to the Father.

But also important here was what had occurred before the event that John was going to describe. The enemy of God

Himself had exercised his influence over Judas to turn Jesus over to the religious authorities, which probably included the pledge to give witness against Christ, as well.

All of this being true, John indicated, "Then He poured water into the basin, and began to wash the disciples' feet, and to wipe them with the towel with which He was girded" (13:5). To say that this would have been shocking to John's first century audience would be an understatement. The washing of someone's feet was left to the individual or more commonly to a slave where possible. This was a lowly, demeaning action. What we have here on the part of Christ was one of the most graphic portrayals or acts of pure, unadulterated humility that could have possibly been done by Jesus, in that He was who He was, which of course, was John's point in framing the action in this manner.

John's understanding and previous interpretation is borne out by Jesus' explanation of Himself to them, when He said,

> And so when He had washed their feet, and taken His garments, and reclined at the table again, He said to them, "Do you know what I have done to you? You call Me Teacher and Lord; and you are right, for so I am. If I then, the Lord and the Teacher, washed your feet, you also ought to wash one another's feet. For I gave you an example that you also should do as I did to you. Truly, truly, I say to you, a slave is not greater than his master; neither is one who is sent greater than the one who sent

him. If you know these things, you are blessed if you do them (13:12-17).

The context of this act by Jesus placed in sharp contrast the fleshliness of the disciples and this act of loving humility in service. This can be seen in Luke's account of what had been taking place during the supper in the upper room just prior to this action of the Savior,

> And there arose also a dispute among them as to which one of them was regarded to be greatest. And He said to them, "The kings of the Gentiles lord it over them; and those who have authority over them are called 'Benefactors.' But not so with you, but let him who is the greatest among you become as the youngest, and the leader as the servant. For who is greater, the one who reclines at the table, or the one who serves? Is it not the one who reclines at the table? But I am among you as the one who serves (Lk. 22:24-27).

Jesus was showing them loving, humble service in the face of their own vying for position and power. This act of humility especially stands out in light of the expulsion of Judas.

### *The Expulsion of Judas*

The actions of Judas had been mentioned immediately by John in his authorial comments in 13:2 regarding the situation that was unfolding here. However, this would not be the only mention of Judas, for he would become a negative thread throughout the opening sections of this discourse; so important, that one would not be able to understand much of this discourse without it. This was a thread of which Jesus was well aware, but of which the disciples were completely clueless.

This negative thread was exposed to the group first by Jesus identifying during the washing of the disciples' feet that there was one among them who was not saved, who had not been cleansed (13:10). John alerted the reader to the fact that this was a reference to the betrayer in their midst, whom he had in fact earlier identified to the reader as Judas.

Judas was mentioned in veiled reference a third time after Jesus washed the disciples' feet and explained what the act meant specifically for them, which was that they should lovingly serve each other in humility. He then said, "I do not speak of all of you. I know the ones I have chosen; but it is that the Scripture may be fulfilled, 'He who eats My bread has lifted up his heel against Me'" (13:18).

Judas was then brought up a fourth time in this opening section, a third time by Christ. While the two earlier references seemed not to stir the disciples, this third mention by Jesus was plain and it was apparently spoken with visible emotion on the part of the Savior. John recorded it in 13:21, "When Jesus had said this, He became troubled in spirit, and testified, and said, 'Truly, truly, I say to you, that one of you will betray Me.'" This time the disciples responded to what they heard. They became concerned about this betrayer that Jesus indicated was within their midst, concerned enough to ask Him who the traitor was (13:22-25). Peter initiated this and probably wanted to take

## THE CONTEXT OF THE PARABLE

care of the traitor himself. Peter was as close to being the muscle of the group as anyone.

Jesus acquiesced somewhat to their desire to find out the person's identity and gave them a means by which they would be able to know who it was, the dipping and giving of the morsel (13:26). But He did more than that, He pointed him out in spoken word, "What you do, do quickly" (13:27).

In spite of these things, the disciples were completely clueless regarding Judas. Notice John's record of what took place after this, "Now no one of those reclining at the table knew for what purpose He had said this to him. For some were supposing, because Judas had the money box, that Jesus was saying to him, 'Buy the things we have need of for the feast'; or else, that he should give something to the poor. And so after receiving the morsel he went out immediately; and it was night" (13:28-30).

They were completely oblivious. If anyone was trustworthy, if anyone was clean, if anyone was truly a follower of Christ, surely it was Judas. The disciples trusted Judas with their very lives, because when it came time to identify someone righteous enough, someone trustworthy enough, someone faithful enough to Jesus' mission to entrust their money, the disciples had selected Judas.

### *The Fixation on the Disciples*

The storyline continues after the removal of Judas with a fixation upon the disciples who remained. Beginning in 13:31 through to 14:31, Jesus expounds upon the fact that He is the only way to the Father. He began in 13:31-38 with the fact that He was going to leave them and that they must express heartfelt love for one another while He was gone, for He said, "By this all men will know that you are My disciples, if you have love for one another" (13:35). Peter expressed the dismay of the entire group over the idea that they no longer would be together in 13:36-38. Jesus made it clear to both him and them, that their desire to be with Him was impossible.

In the next section, John recorded how Jesus reinforced the fact of this matter by telling them where He was actually going to go, "In My Father's house are many dwelling places; if it were not so, I would have told you; for I go to prepare a place for you" (14:2). He was returning to the Father and this should not produce fear and dismay, as they were evidencing, but rather faith and trust (14:1). The reason He was departing was for their benefit, as such they would join Him later, the way being paved for them. "Jesus said to him, 'I am the way, and the truth, and the life; no one comes to the Father, but through Me'" (14:6).

Of course, this entire discussion and its trajectory would have raised questions in the minds of the disciples. In anticipation of their questions, Jesus answered why He was going and why He was the only way to get to where He was going (14:7-15). He had come to do something that He had concluded and now the relationship with the Father was to be restored to its previous character with benefits for His followers, "Believe Me that I am in the Father, and the Father in Me; otherwise believe on account of the works themselves. Truly, truly, I say to you, he who believes in Me, the works that I do shall he do

## THE CONTEXT OF THE PARABLE

also; and greater works than these shall he do; because I go to the Father" (14:11-12).

How will all of this take place on the behalf of the disciples? The final section deals with just such a reality, focusing upon both the character and the function of the Holy Spirit, "And I will ask the Father, and He will give you another Helper, that He may be with you forever; that is, the Spirit of truth, whom the world cannot receive, because it does not behold Him or know Him, but you know Him because He abides with you, and will be in you" (14:16-17). As Jesus drew His opening comments on the matter of His leaving to a close, we see a summary of the various ideas He had communicated to them expressed just prior to John 15,

> Peace I leave with you; My peace I give to you; not as the world gives, do I give to you. Let not your heart be troubled, nor let it be fearful. You heard that I said to you, 'I go away, and I will come to you.' If you loved Me, you would have rejoiced, because I go to the Father; for the Father is greater than I. And now I have told you before it comes to pass, that when it comes to pass, you may believe. I will not speak much more with you, for the ruler of the world is coming, and he has nothing in Me; but that the world may know that I love the Father, and as the Father gave Me commandment, even so I do. Arise, let us go from here (14:27-31).

## LIFE IN THE VINE

These words lead us into Jesus' first use of a metaphor within the discourse with the words, "I am the true vine, and My Father is the vinedresser" (15:1).

## 2
# The Metaphor of the Vine

*For the vineyard of the LORD of hosts*
*is the house of Israel, And the men of Judah*
*His delightful plant. Thus He looked for justice,*
*but behold, bloodshed; For righteousness,*
*but behold, a cry of distress.*
*Isaiah 5:7*

Anyone who has spent any amount of time within a local church has passed through the cycle of hope and despair that accompanies the public decisions of people to follow Christ. Although my present church does not have altar calls, I grew up in a church that did and I often witnessed former members who I had not seen in a while come back and reconnect with the church. Sometimes it was said that they had lost their salvation and had been saved again. Other times it was indicated that they had rededicated their lives to the Lord. It would not be until many years later that I would sort out much of what was going on, but many of us remember this type of activity within our local church bodies.

Our tendency as humans is to consider any decision or religious act by a person to be legitimate. After all, we think, what gives me the right to question the authenticity of someone else? But this mindset is contradicted by the reason for Jesus' communication of the parable of the vine. Jesus spoke this parable within a broader context, a context that included one of the most villainous figures in human history, Judas. A man who decided to follow Jesus, who answered His call, but was nonetheless not a genuine believer.

As the reader approaches the fifteenth chapter of John and the metaphor of the vine, they are presented with a little bit of a challenge. There does not seem to be a connection between the upcoming and preceding division. Let us examine this a little closer.

These divisions of Jesus' comments seem to be in severe disjunction from each other. First, there is no verbal connection made between the previous division and this upcoming one. Second, there seems to be no direct connection with the focus of the content of these divisions. The previous division clearly focused upon the idea of Jesus leaving and of them coming to join Him, while this upcoming division focused upon the validity of the disciple. So, was Jesus just picking up another idea that He wanted to address with them before He departed? This could definitely be the case, except that there are a couple verbal and conceptual ties between what has been said.

## The Metaphor of the Vine

### *The Purpose of the Division*

First, Jesus speaks of the disciples as a group under the designation of being clean in 15:3. This takes the reader back to Jesus' opening action in this division of the book and the controversial act of washing the disciples' feet. A second connection is the mention of the word of Christ and what it accomplished in the disciples, which we find mentioned in the previous section. These two realities, along with the emphasis on the validity of the disciple, points the reader to the connection between what Jesus was going to address at the beginning of John 15 and the issue of Judas. One of the most difficult things to make sense of within the Christian church is the existence of people like Judas within its midst. The opening of John 15 was meant to provide a means of comprehending just such situations.

The story of Judas was the story of a man, who not only was close to Christ in a personal sense, but he was a witness to the authentic workings of God not only through Christ, but even more powerfully, within the lives of other people. Judas was completely accepted by all of the disciples as a follower of Jesus. He had an immediate experience of spiritual matters. They thought of him in positive ways and felt no concern to watch or keep their eyes upon him. After all, he carried the financial resources of the traveling team.

Because of Jesus' concern for the disciples, particularly in light of His leaving, it was critical for Him to give the rest of the disciples and those who would follow them, a way in which they might be able to make sense of this type of situation.

Without these words of Jesus in John 15, the disciples would have had no framework for understanding Judas' behavior. However, in spite of the spiritual experiences and closeness to the spiritual realities of Christ, he could still not be a part of their group and was never a part of it in the first place.

This is played out rather graphically in John 13. As noted earlier, throughout the opening sequence of that chapter, Jesus came back to Judas time and time again, describing first his problem, He had not experienced the cleansing of being washed spiritually by Jesus (13:10-11), then the ultimate reason for his problem, unlike the other disciples, he had not been chosen by Christ (13:18), and then finally the consequence of his problem, the betrayal of Christ (13:21). This was to no avail, because even when Jesus identified him specifically by action in 13:26-30, they still refused to believe that Judas was not faithful to Christ.

However, after Judas left, notice the description of Jesus under the influence and guidance of the Holy Spirit, "When therefore he had gone out, Jesus said, 'Now is the Son of Man glorified, and God is glorified in Him; if God is glorified in Him, God will also glorify Him in Himself, and will glorify Him immediately'" (13:31-32).

You see here the critical nature of Judas' exit. Notice the words "When," "therefore," "Now is," and "immediately," all which point to its critical nature. Jesus was waiting for the exit of Judas to address some matters with the disciples that definitively applied to them. But even so, the eleven were in no way under the impression that these words did not also apply to Judas. Jesus was the only person at that moment in time that realized that the words He was now speaking after Judas' exodus had no application whatsoever for Judas, but only the eleven.

In fact, it could be said, due to the dominance of Judas throughout the opening section, that the actions of Jesus in washing the disciples' feet, as well as the words that He chose to explain those actions, were all geared towards the expulsion of Judas from their midst. This fits the context and also properly supports both the transition of John and the words of Jesus that appear in 13:31-32.

Jesus on His final night with the disciples before His crucifixion desired to only address those who could fit the description given in His prayer for them, "I manifested Thy name to the men whom Thou gavest Me out of the world; Thine they were, and Thou gavest them to Me, and they have kept Thy word" (17:6). It is interesting in this regard that the very first way that Jesus addressed the eleven once Judas was removed from their midst was "Little children" (13:33). This address was not true until Judas had left their midst.

*The Meaning of the Metaphor*

So, with the exit of Judas from the midst of Jesus' true followers, in the beginning section of John 15 Jesus addressed the matter of how the disciples in specific and believers in general might be able to identify those within their midst who were only believers in appearance, but were not so in actual reality. In order to rivet home to them His point, Jesus used a metaphor which graphically pictured the contrast between the true follower of Christ and the counterfeit one, and in doing so communicated the essence of the Christian experience or Christian life, if you would. Jesus said,

> I am the true vine, and My Father is the vinedresser. Every branch in Me that does not bear fruit, He takes away; and every branch that bears fruit, He prunes it, that it may bear more fruit. You are already clean because of the word which I have spoken to you. Abide in Me, and I in you. As the branch cannot bear fruit of itself, unless it abides in the vine, so neither can you, unless you abide in Me. I am the vine, you are the branches; he who abides in Me, and I in him, he bears much fruit; for apart from Me you can do nothing. If anyone does not abide in Me, he is thrown away as a branch, and dries up; and they gather them, and cast them into the fire, and they are burned. If you abide in Me, and My words abide in you, ask whatever you wish, and it shall be done for you. By this is My Father glorified, that you bear much fruit, and so prove to be My disciples. Just as the Father has loved Me, I have also loved you; abide in My love. If you keep My commandments, you will abide in My love; just as I have kept My Father's commandments, and abide in His love. These things I have spoken to you, that My joy may be in you, and that your joy may be made full (15:1-11).

The metaphor is that of the vine and the branches.

## THE METAPHOR OF THE VINE

The vine was an important crop in the ancient world, for not only did it provide fruit to eat, but more importantly, it supplied the main liquid used for drink in the ancient world, its juice, that often was consumed in the form of wine. Like the other crops, God's stipulations are presented throughout the Old Testament on how the vine was to be cared for and how its fruit, usually in the form of wine, was to be used within the social and religious system of Israel. It was treated within the instructions of God having to do with fruit trees. So, for example, the fruit tree and/or vine fell under several regulations in the Pentateuch.

When a city was being sieged for conquest, the fruit trees could not be cut down (Deut. 20:19-20). Yahweh specifically commanded the nation to plant fruit trees (Lev. 19:23). Once planted they could not eat from it until the fifth year of its produce (Lev. 19:23-25). The fruit from a vineyard was so important that God allowed a man that had been drafted into warfare to return home and not have to fight if he had not had the privilege of eating of the first fruit from it (Deut. 20:6). Like the grain crops, unharvested portions were to be left for the poor (Lev. 19:9-10). God also laid out the process for the bearing of fruit. The best way to understand this process would be to divide it into the initial or non-repetitive step and the repetitive step.

The initial step was a two-pronged process which included the construction of the vineyard or orchard and the planting of the fruit bearing vines or trees that would be grown there. The construction would be as simple as a bramble/brier/thorny bush fence (cf. Isa. 5:5; Prov. 15:19) and as complicated as a stone wall (cf. Prov. 24:31; Isa. 5:5). The more elaborate vineyards might have had a watchtower from which the full expanse of it might be safely guarded (cf. Prov. 27:18; Isa. 5:2; 27:2-3).

If a watchtower was not part of the construction, then some type of temporary structure, to protect mostly from the heat and inclement weather, would have been available for the owner to stay in during ripening season so that he could effectively guard his property (cf. Isa. 1:8; 4:6).[1] The stones for much of this construction would have come from the ground that was to be used for the planting. This leads to the second prong in this initial step.

The ground had to be cleared of all bushes and stones, which allowed for the planting of the vines or the trees.[2] The planting stage required care in order to guarantee that enough room was left for effective cultivation and harvesting. This became particularly important in reference to the grapevine which required ongoing care to yield a goodly amount of fruit. This leads to the second step or the repetitive step.

In the repetitive step there were two methods used in the cultivation of the grape. One method allowed the vines to lie and spread upon the ground being directed by laid stones.[3] The second method was to train the vine through pruning to grow up and between trees or poles to create a canopy effect.[4] Branches that did not grow in the direction intended by the vinedresser were pruned, cut off, thus allowing for controlled growth and direction. This second method allowed for easier harvesting, as well as easier cultivation since a plow could be used between the base of the vines and not just a hand hoe as in the case of the vine being allowed to spread on the ground.[5]

However, the hand hoe would have been used in conjunction with the plow even in this method because one would not have wanted to use a plow close to the base of the vine, or would not have been able to use it close to the surrounding wall either.[6] The pruning of the vine was a consistent concern for the vinedresser. Removing useless branches or excess foliage, as well as placing poorly growing branches in the sunlight allowed for the maximum growth of the vine.[7]

Having prepared the ground and planted the crops, the farmer would tend to them, looking forward to the time of harvest. The harvest time was a time of great joy and happiness. The first step in the harvesting process was reaping. Like most agricultural pursuits in ancient Israel the method of reaping was dependent on the size of one's field and upon that which was being reaped.

The reaping process for fruit crops depended, of course, upon the type of fruit plant or tree. In the case of the grape, the reaping involved picking the bunches of grapes and placing them into a vessel for transfer to the winepress.[8] After the fruit had been gathered through the reaping process, the next step in the process prepared the harvested product for its final stage of refinement and eventual storage. The vineyard and orchard crops went through a pressing process or a drying process.

The harvested grapes would be taken and placed in the winepress, the grapes would then be trod upon, and the juice collected in a receptacle of some sort as the juice drained out of the bottom of the press.[9] There were three different types of winepresses used for this process.[10] One type of winepress was that which was in the vineyard itself or in its vicinity, which would have been hewn out of the rock (cf. Isa. 5:2; Joel. 2:24). The second type of press was that which was constructed from rock and mortar and was usually found within the boundaries of the city. The third type of winepress was a portable winepress, smaller than the second type, having the ability to be moved around. Each of these winepresses allowed two or more people to stand in the press and tread the grapes. This was a time of great rejoicing and celebration.[11]

Grape juice needed to go through a certain process for it to be effectively stored. However, if the juice was to be consumed immediately, then no other process was needed. In order to be able to store grape juice for prolonged periods of time it had to be fermented and made into wine. This process took some time.

The first part of this process was the initial fermenting process which allowed the heavier aspects of the liquid to settle on the bottom of the collection containers. The wine was then gently siphoned off of those containers and placed in wine jars, which were sealed with clay. In order to allow the gases to escape during this final fermenting process, a small hole was left in the jar close to the top that had been sealed.[12]

This process took place in hewn cellars to allow for the constant regulation of the temperature necessary to allow full fermentation to take place.[13] Once the wine was fully fermented then the little hole near the top of the jar was sealed off with a small amount of wet clay.[14] It should also be noted at this point that the grape juice was also used for making a syrup and or a vinegar product.[15]

This is quite a process from the beginning to the end, is it not? An example from the Scriptures should help solidify these processes in one's mind and illustrate how they came together to illustrate spiritual truths within the Scriptures. Take for example Isaiah 5:1-7,

> Let me sing now for my well-beloved A song of my beloved concerning His vineyard. My well-beloved had a vineyard on a fertile hill. And He dug it all around, removed its stones, And planted it with the choicest vine. And He built a tower in the middle of it, And hewed out a wine vat in it; Then He expected it to produce good grapes, But it produced only worthless ones. "And now, O inhabitants of Jerusalem and men of Judah, Judge between Me and My vineyard. What more was there to do for My vineyard that I have not done in it? Why, when I expected it to produce good grapes did it produce worthless ones? So now let Me tell you what I am going to do to My vineyard: I will remove its hedge and it will be consumed; I will break down its wall and it will become trampled ground. And I will lay it waste; It will not be pruned or hoed, But briars and thorns will come up. I will also charge the clouds to rain no rain on it." For the vineyard of the Lord of hosts is the house of Israel, And the men of Judah His delightful plant. Thus He looked for justice, but behold,

bloodshed; For righteousness, but behold, a cry of distress (Isa. 5:1-7).

Here God likened Israel to a vineyard full of grapevines. In fact, God used this imagery of the grapevine throughout the Old Testament to define or describe Israel (Ps. 80:9-16; Isa. 27:2-6; Jer. 2:21:12:10; Ezek. 15:1-8; 17:1-21; 19:10-14; Hos. 10:1, 2). However, rather than accomplishing God's design for them as His servants, they had utterly and completely failed, not producing any fruit, justice and righteousness. What would be the result of this?

Well, even in the Old Testament God indicated that He would send His Servant, who would accomplish what Israel, who was also His servant, little "s", had failed to do. Of this coming Servant the Scriptures indicate, "Behold, My Servant, whom I uphold; My chosen one in whom My soul delights. I have put My Spirit upon Him; He will bring forth justice to the nations" (Isa. 42:1). The justice God had looked for from His vineyard, Israel His servant, but had not found, His future Servant, Jesus, would bring with Him and extend it not just to Israel, but even to the nations.

But this future Servant would not just accomplish what Israel could not accomplish, He in fact would Himself be designated or called, Israel. This becomes clear in the following prophecy of Isaiah, in which this coming Servant will minister to Israel, and, would also be called Israel,

> Listen to Me, O islands, And pay attention, you peoples from afar. The Lord called Me from the womb; From

the body of My mother He named Me. And He has made My mouth like a sharp sword; In the shadow of His hand He has concealed Me, And He has also made Me a select arrow; He has hidden Me in His quiver. And He said to Me, "You are My Servant, Israel, In Whom I will show My glory" . . . He says, "It is too small a thing that You should be My Servant To raise up the tribes of Jacob, and to restore the preserved ones of Israel; I will also make You a light of the nations So that My salvation may reach to the end of the earth" (Isa. 49:1-3, 6).

The fact that the Servant of God was referred to as Israel supports the New Testament reality that aspects of Israel's history were applied directly to Christ by the biblical authors, demonstrating that Christ, in some sense takes the place of Israel as the mechanism of blessing to the nations.

An obvious example of this in the New Testament appeared at the beginning of Matthew's gospel after Joseph fled to Egypt with Mary and Jesus on the counsel of an angelic messenger (2:13). Matthew, under the inspiration of the Holy Spirit, concluded this with the following words, "And he arose and took the Child and His mother by night, and departed for Egypt; and was there until the death of Herod, that what was spoken by the Lord through the prophet might be fulfilled, saying, 'Out of Egypt did I call My Son'" (2:14-15). The out of Egypt statement was a quote directly from Hosea 11:1, which was spoken to the nation of Israel.

Here we see, then, the escalation of the identity of both the Servant of God and the Son of God meeting in the person of Jesus. This is played out in the words of John 15:1, "I am the true vine, and My Father is the vinedresser." Unlike the failures of the nation of Israel, the vine of God in the Old Testament, Jesus, the true vine, will accomplish what they could never do. He will produce righteousness in those who were a part of the vine; and it was that righteousness, that is, fruit bearing, that John so powerfully addressed.

One of the most critical passages on the Christian life found within the teachings of the New Testament is found in the fifteenth chapter of the gospel of John. The context of this statement made by Jesus Christ was the Upper Room Discourse, the last time of teaching and interaction with the disciples before Jesus was crucified. After Judas was dismissed to carry out his betrayal of Christ, Jesus focused intently upon the disciples, preparing them for His looming departure. This preparation included some guidance on the matter of how to make sense of the abandonment of the group by one of the most trustworthy men among their ranks, Judas, the disciple chosen to carry the group's financial resources. To expose the apostasy of Judas theologically, Jesus turned to the matter of fruitfulness.

# 3
# The Role of the Father and Son in Your Fruitfulness

*I am the true vine,
and My Father is the vinedresser.
John 15:1*

As a pastor I have often found myself in my office sitting across from a dear believer who was wrestling with some aspect of his Christian experience that he did not believe matched up with what he read in the Scriptures. Whether it is marriage problems, decisions he must make, or his own spiritual or ethical lifestyle, I find myself having to both exhort and comfort at the same time.

You see, a fact of the matter is that while we never really are where we desire to be as believers in our spiritual depth and strength, it is not all up to us to be so. My spirituality is not just a matter of me, alone. In fact, true spiritual maturity both starts and ends with God. It is based on the working of God in a preliminary sense and its for the glory of God in its ultimate end. We just show up in the middle, responding to

God's work and being a conduit of His grace. This comes to the forefront in the very beginning of the parable of the vine.

Jesus commenced His discussion of spiritual fruitfulness with the role of God the Father and God the Son in this spiritual reality. Spiritual fruitfulness is not a human matter alone. Although fruitfulness takes place in humans, it is not because of humans. The ultimate cause of fruitfulness is a divine issue. In 15:1-2 Jesus opened up His analysis of fruitfulness with an explanation of its context. He elaborated on both the divine participants (15:1) and the human participants (15:2) in the fruit bearing process. Before examining the participants, the absence of the Spirit in the process must be addressed.

## *The Spirit's Role Assumed*

It seemed strange that Christ did not refer to the Holy Spirit's role at all as a participant in this process. This is even stranger given the fact that the Holy Spirit was presented as playing such a vital and integral role in spiritual growth in the theology of the apostle Paul.

However, the strangeness vanishes when these words are understood in their broader context within the Upper Room Discourse. Just a chapter earlier Jesus had made the following statement regarding the Spirit,

> And I will ask the Father, and He will give you another Helper, that He may be with you forever; that is the Spirit of truth, whom the world cannot receive, because

it does not behold Him or know Him, but you know Him because He abides with you, and will be in you. I will not leave you as orphans; I will come to you. After a little while the world will behold Me no more; but you will behold Me; because I live, you shall live also (14:16-19).

What these words make plain is that possessing the Spirit was considered by Jesus to be the same as possessing Him, Christ, because the Spirit was "another Helper" and as such He must be understood as Christ's abiding presence in them (14:16-19).

In conjunction with this, Jesus indicated that the Spirit was to bring back to the disciples' memory all that Jesus had said (14:26). But this is not all, for in the next chapter, John 16, Jesus will indicate that the Spirit's role was not to act on His own accord, but to solely glorify Christ (16:13-15). What these truths lead us to conclude is that if Christ was to be involved then He would do so through the Holy Spirit being involved.

## *Christ's Role*

In John 15:1a, regarding His own role, Christ said, "I am the true vine." Christ obviously used a metaphor here, that is, a visual picture, to expound on the issue of fruitfulness. The metaphor of the vine was a common biblical example. The grapevine was a common fixture in the landscape of Jesus' day. They were grown all over the land of Israel. Its foliage was extensive, providing shade for its owner. But it was not its foliage in which man was interested but rather its fruit. The vine was the source of five different products.

The grapes were eaten just as they were from the vine. The grapes could be dried and made into raisins to be preserved for later consumption. Raisins were also pressed into cakes for easy storage and transport. Juice could be made by treading the grapes in a wine press. But by far the most desired product of the grape was the wine that would be produced by allowing the juice to ferment. The fruitfulness and benefit of the grapevine led to its use in the communication of the concept of prosperity and material blessing in biblical literature.

Several biblical examples illustrate this fact. The twelve spies brought back signs of the prosperity of the Promised Land, one branch from a vine that was so laden with grapes that it had to be carried between two men on a pole (Num. 13:23). Micah 4:4 phrases the prosperity of living in God's kingdom in the following fashion, "And each of them will sit under his vine and under his fig tree, with no one to make them afraid, for the mouth of the Lord of hosts has spoken" (cf. Zech. 3:10). But if the vine was the ultimate symbol of prosperity, it was also the ultimate sign of God's judgment.

The winepress in which the grapes were trodden to extract their juice became the symbol of the place of God's execution of His judgment on mankind in both the Old Testament (Isa. 63:1-3) and the New Testament (Rev. 14:18-20). In keeping with this symbolism, if the winepress was the place of judgment, then the vintage wine that such a judgment produced was the wrath of God, for Jeremiah 25:15 said, "For thus the Lord, the God of Israel, says to me, 'Take this cup of the wine of wrath from My hand, and cause all the nations, to whom I send you, to drink it.'"

But it is to neither the symbol of prosperity or the symbol of judgment that Christ referred when He called Himself the vine. It was to a much richer image that Christ was speaking. As noted in the previous chapter, in the Old and New Testaments the nation of Israel is referred to as God's vine. Although this comparison is an extensive one in the Old Testament appearing in Psalms, Jeremiah, Ezekiel, Hosea, and other books, the most classic reference appeared in the passage that served as an example previously in Isaiah 5:1-7.

In that passage God was said to have taken the time to prepare the vineyard and the soil for the vines and then ordered the best vines He could. But at the end of 5:2 it said, "Then He expected it to produce good grapes, but it produced only worthless ones." For that reason it had to be judged, because as 5:4 asked, "What more was there to do for My vineyard that I have not done in it?"

Jesus picked up on this same motif or theme in Matthew 21:33-46. He was there telling a parable to the religious leaders that would indicate the source and extent of His authority. 21:33 began with a deliberate reference and then quotation of Isaiah 5:1-2, but adds that the vineyard was rented out to growers, while the owner went away on a journey. These growers would be responsible for making the vines produce fruit.

When it became time to collect the harvest of grapes in 21:34 the owner sent a group of slaves who were mistreated and killed (21:35). This same thing happened with a second group

(21:36). Then in desperation the owner sent his own son, whom the growers decided to kill, that they might be able to get the produce for themselves (21:37-39). Jesus asked a question to the listeners regarding what the owner would do when he came, to which they promptly answered, "They said to Him, 'He will bring those wretches to a wretched end, and will rent out the vineyard to other vine-growers, who will pay him the proceeds at the proper seasons'" (21:41).

They were so engrossed in the story that they did not even realize that they were pronouncing judgment on themselves, which Jesus indicated. Jesus was the rejected son, the religious leaders were the growers, and only through Him could kingdom access be gained (21:42-46).

This is to what Jesus was ultimately referring. Israel and Israel's leaders had failed in their responsibilities to produce the proper fruit of God, that is, the justice and righteousness that were identified in Isaiah 5, those things God was looking for from His vine when He came to investigate its readiness for harvest. As such, Christ said, "I am the true vine." Jesus has taken the place of Israel. Now, men must come unto Him if they want access to God through salvation. He is the ultimate validator of the reception of life. Christ said, He was the vine. He would produce in men that to which Israel was supposed to be the conduit.

He called Himself the true vine, "true" being the Greek word *alethinos*. This Greek term referred to something being "authentic." Inherent in this term was a comparison, that is, this is real and that is not. Such was born out in its secular uses which included comparing real racial groups with what seemed to be such, or real costly garments with imitations. Christ was subsuming all aspects of what Israel was to accomplish to Himself. He would now become the guarantor of these things.

Israel and its leaders had been set aside and He was taking their place as God's representative and God's channel to Himself. It would be through Him, the ultimate seed of the woman and the ultimate seed of Abraham, that all the families of the earth would be blessed, including, by the way, Israel (Gen. 3:15; 22:17-18; Gal. 3:16). Even Israel, although not losing its most favored nation status, would now have to come to God through Christ, or miss out on God altogether. But not only was there a vine, there was also a vinedresser in this new situation.

## *The Father's Role*

Christ said, "and My Father is the vinedresser" (15:1b). The vinedresser is the one who cares for the vine. This required a wide range of skills and efforts in the ancient world. This person had to have masonry skills to be able to build the stone walls surrounding the vineyard, the stone winepress, and if possible the stone watchtower from which to guard his precious commodity. He had to understand the seasons of growth and exactly when to prune, fertilize, and till. The vinedresser managed the growth and fruit bearing potential of the vine.

This statement by Jesus, identifying the Father as the vinedresser, provided a strategic connection to the main Old Testament passage, Isaiah 5:1-7, which served as a parallel to this idea here. Although the word vinedresser was not used in that passage, clearly God was presented within that particular function. He did everything from building the structures associated with the vineyard, preparing the soil and planting the vine, as well as cultivating and harvesting the produce. The connections should be obvious.

The truth that the Father is the ultimate source of growth in the body and the members of it is a truth that the Scripture expresses in various ways, using various imagery. One such interesting passage occurs within Paul's discussion of spiritual gifts set within the broader context of true spirituality in 1 Corinthians 12-14. In 1 Corinthians 12:6, Paul states, "And there are varieties of effects, but the same God who works all things in all persons." What makes this statement particularly appealing to grasping the Father's role is the inclusion within the context of the two other members of the Godhead, "Now there are varieties of gifts, but the same Spirit. And there are varieties of ministries, and the same Lord" (12:4-5).

What is Paul's point here? Having established a condition of caution among the Corinthians, alerting them to the reality of the existence of counterfeit spiritual gifts in 12:1-3, Paul transitions into a discussion of true or legitimate spiritual gifts. In the next eight verses, the apostle gives a concise overview of the basic set of truths regarding spiritual gifts, particularly their source, purpose, and nature. This summary is clearly divided into three sections. 12:4-7 gives the placement of the gifts within the divine program for the church. 12:8-10 produces a sampling of the types of gifts given to the church. 12:11 summarizes the overriding message of the two previous sections.

## THE ROLE OF THE FATHER AND SON IN YOUR FRUITFULNESS

Beyond the general truths regarding gifts that are introduced with these verses, Paul further introduces some key ideas that will be useful throughout this section: the variety of gifts, their intention to benefit the entire body, and the consensus between the members of the Trinity regarding them. This third point is the one to consider in the matter of the Father's role in the matter of spiritual fruitfulness.

In 1 Corinthians 12:4 Paul focuses upon the Spirit, indicating, "Now there are varieties of gifts, but the same Spirit." The fact that there are multiple allotments of gifts in no way demands that there also be a multiple number of Spirits. There exists only one Spirit. However, Paul says more than just there being one Spirit, his point is more importantly the "same" Spirit. The idea of the same Spirit communicates something more significant than just the idea one Spirit does.

The idea of same stands in a clearer contrast to the idea of difference and diversity which is the point he is hammering home to the Corinthians. Diversity is in perfect harmony with the Spirit, not in contention with Him. In other words, the divergence that is manifested in spiritual gifts is a purposeful accomplishment by the Spirit for the benefit of the body and not for rank, competition, rivalry, and showy escapades. The next verse continues Paul's thought.

In this text, Paul is framing his discussion regarding the source and purpose of spiritual gifts around the Trinity. Having commented on gifts and the Holy Spirit, Paul now comments on the Lord and ministries. Paul writes, "And there are varieties of ministries, and the same Lord" (12:5). The gifts are given to the saints for the purpose of executing ministries. But, who are the objects of the ministries themselves?

The object of the ministries are the saints themselves. It is a major point throughout these three chapters that the ministries that are carried out in the strength of these gifts are directed towards the body (cf. 12:7, 25). Note also the words of Ephesians 4:12 in this regard of ministry by the saints being, "for the work of service, to the building up of the body of Christ." The church as the body of Christ is a major theme throughout this section and it is to this body that ministry guided and fueled by the gifts, takes place.

So, the ultimate object of ministries of the saints is the Lord, as to their object. Just because there are different ministries being executed for the Lord's benefit, does not mean different Lords, but rather that the Lord, as the Holy Spirit, is concerned with diversity.

In the following verse Paul added two more truths to the four that he has already established in 12:4-6. He says in 12:6, "And there are varieties of effects, but the same God who works all things in all persons." To varieties of gifts and ministries is added a multiplicity of "effects." The idea of "effect" is translated from the Greek word *energema*, which is related to the Greek term from which we derive the English word energy. It referred to an action accomplished, something that is brought about or wrought, that is, a work done. This variety in no way impinges upon there being the same God. In this way, this verse seems quite similar to the other two that have preceded it. However, Paul does something different with this verse.

### THE ROLE OF THE FATHER AND SON IN YOUR FRUITFULNESS

Unlike in the previous verses, the member of the Trinity is described in this verse. He is the one who "works all things in all persons." The word "works" is the verb of the noun "effects" in the previous clause, *energeo*. The "effects" of which there exists a variety are all accomplished by the same God. The wording of these clauses indicates that they are in fact linked to each other and that this concept of the same God accomplishing the variety of effects is actually the truth.

This reality of the Father's work in the church is taught not just in this passage, but in other verses in the New Testament. For example, Paul remarked in 1 Corinthians 3:6-7, "I planted, Apollos watered, but God was causing the growth. So then neither the one who plants nor the one who waters is anything, but God who causes the growth." So, the connection that is made between these two clauses affirms what was said about the previous two verses. In other words, just as the same God controls the multiple effects, the same Lord controls the multiple ministries, and the same Spirit controls the multiple gifts.

What becomes clear from this passage is that although all the members of the Godhead are engaged in the life, ministry, and growth of the church, it is the Father who is the ultimate source of the spiritual fruitfulness towards which the Godhead works within the body.

Through this opening statement, Jesus has laid out several important truths. First, He has indicated that He and not the nation is the ultimate channel of life and access to God. This should not be seen as an abandoning of Israel, but a proper elevation of her rightful Ruler and promised Savior. Second, Jesus has clearly identified Himself as the source from which life is drawn. The grapevine does not draw its life from the branches that compose it, but rather the branches that compose it draw their life from the vine.

Third, Jesus identified Himself in this text as the totality of the plant, that is the spiritual entity He was identifying, not simply the trunk of it. This is somewhat of a departure from other imagery, where Jesus was pictured as a cornerstone or foundation of a structure. This indicates that Jesus was referring to something bigger than just the church, but the totality of that which God is building or growing throughout salvation history.

A fourth truth that flows necessarily out of the previous is that Jesus is the one to whom everybody must be connected if growth is going to occur. Yes, He is the totality of the plant, but in spite of that fact one can be an actual part of that plant if they are properly connected to Him. Fifth, God the Father is the one who maximizes the growth potential of the vine. He is the vinedresser, growth is His responsibility, the result of His work, and the channel through which that growth will occur is Christ.

This last fact, here, leads to a rather ominous point that must be realized, the sixth point. The growth potential of the vine, since the vine is Jesus, who is divine, is limitless and the expertise of the vinedresser is limitless since the vinedresser is God. What this means then, seventhly, is if growth does not take place it cannot be the fault of or an issue with either the vine or the vinedresser. They are blameless when it comes to no growth taking place, that is justice and righteousness, and worthy of all the praise when growth does take place.

# 4
# The Fact of Fruitlessness in the Church

*Every branch in Me that does not*
*bear fruit, He takes away . . .*
*John 15:2a*

Is it possible to lose one's salvation? This question has been a constant source of debate within the church, with various camps at various times in church history holding to these separate perspectives. When a person within the church lacks fruit is that a sign that they were not saved in the first place or a sign that they might have lost their salvation? Although there is not a singular passage where these ideas can be definitively answered, people do argue one point or another from this text. What does this passage truly teach on this issue?

In discussing the human side of the growth process, Jesus mentioned the possibility of two different scenarios. Within the context of the spiritual entity we know as the church, there could be a fruitless branch and a fruitful branch. This affirmation by Jesus has been the source of much contention and confusion over the years, so it will be challenging to understand His point.

## *The Fact of Fruitless Branches*

The first type of branch that Jesus mentioned was the fruitless branch. Maintaining His metaphor of the vine and the vinedresser, Jesus said, "Every branch in Me that does not bear fruit, He takes away" (15:2a). A problem is found in the fruit bearing of some branches. Some do not "bear fruit," Jesus said. It should be noted that it was not the scarcity of fruit that Jesus found problematic, but the absence of it entirely.

The verb "bear" used by John to reflect Jesus' expression was the Greek term *pheiro*. It had many senses, but its four primary meanings were: 1) bear in the sense of carrying something; 2) bear in the sense of moving something out of position, as in the wind was bearing along the boat; 3) bear in the sense of bringing on something, as in he came bearing some food to eat; and 4) bear in the sense of producing something, that is bringing something forth. It is this last sense that John used to express the intended meaning of Jesus. Thus, the first type of branch discussed by Christ was not producing, bringing forth from itself, "fruit."

The term "fruit" was obviously a figure of speech for something of manifoldly greater significance. Vines bring forth grapes, but grapes were not an issue here because from 15:1 the vine was Christ and the vinedresser was God. By implication at least the branch was someone related to Christ (In what way, will depend on a proper interpretation). The fruit would then be that which the life that is in Christ necessarily produces in those properly attached to Him.

Grapevines produce grapes, apple trees produce apples, fig trees produce figs, and they do so necessarily. In other words, the grapevine must produce grapes due to the nature of the plant that it is. But, it must also produce grapes of necessity because it is living. If a vine has life in it, such a reality will of necessity produce fruit and that fruit will of necessity be grapes. Failure to bring forth fruit exposes the plant as having an absence of properly working life in it.

Given these facts, then, the question is, what does the Christ vine produce? Well, the life that springs from Christ according to John's gospel leads to walking in the light (8:12), to eternal life (6:53-54; 11:25), and to knowing God (17:3). Romans 6:22 indicates that the fruit that we derive is "sanctification" which ultimately ends up in eternal life. James calls fruit, in 3:18 of his letter, the fruit of righteousness. *Fruit here, as it is used by Jesus, is a life characterized by a vitality of Spirit produced qualities, which are defined and expressed by faithfulness in belief and conduct towards Christ and His teachings.* The definition will be validated as we work our way through the passage.

This being true, it can be confidently said that the branch, which was barren of fruit, was not walking in the light, was not growing in intimacy with God, was not living a life marked by sanctification, was not living a life of righteousness, and was not reflecting Christ in its overall direction and manner. It was fruitless, void of spiritual vitality. So, this fruit which was expected, given the nature of the vine and the nature of the vinedresser, was absent. No wonder the branch was said to be taken away. What does any worthwhile vinedresser do when a branch clearly manifests the fact that it does not possess the life of the vine in it, that is, that it is in fact dead? He takes it away. Why? Because it absorbs nutrients unnecessarily.

This concept comes from the Greek word *airo* and means to either "lift up," "lift, in order to carry," or "to carry off." The last two have quite a threatening implication, such as, carried off where? Some commentators argue that the meaning here was simply "lift up" so as to get more sunlight and better care. This is difficult to prove given what Jesus was going to say of the branch in 15:6. So a full conclusion as to what this lifting referred to will have to wait until 15:6. A few preliminary observations can be made, however.

At minimum, this is a very perverse situation. A branch, seemingly attached to the very epicenter of life itself, carefully worked on by God the Father, Himself, that does not produce that same life that is in the vine? This is at minimum, freakish. But was there something deeper going on here? Was Jesus actually saying that this branch was really connected to Him, or just that it seemed to be connected to Him?

This really gets down to the difficulties associated with interpreting this passage accurately. Was this first branch to be understood to be a Christian, or was it simply a supposed Christian, a Christian or follower of Christ in name only? Was Jesus saying that there are some persons attached to the church that do not bear fruit and as a result of such will be eventually exposed to be such? Was the taking away to be understood as a loss of salvation, or a placement in a context of where growth could take place, or a loss of rewards, or something else entirely?

## The Identity of Fruitless Branches

These types of questions and many more have plagued this verse and its interpretation for years. Many of the problems, although not all of them, hinge upon one's interpretation of the prepositional phrase "in Me" at the beginning of the statement. There are two distinct possibilities for understanding how this phrase was being used by John in the recording of Jesus' statement to the disciples.

### Practically Speaking

In the Greek language, there is not an unbending word order to communicate grammatical relationships as we do in the English language. As such, word order was flexible and words could appear anywhere in the sentence, because grammatical markers were part of the word itself. If an author wanted to emphasize a particular word or concept, he would move that word or phrase to the very front of the sentence.

The phrase "in Me" appears at the very front of the sentence in the Greek text, not after the word "branch", as reflected in our English translation. Therefore, its grammatical relationship must be discovered by way of interpretation, since it could be modifying either the noun "branch" or the verbal concept of "bear fruit." In other words, it is either adjectival or adverbial in its focus.

If this phrase modified "branch" then it would be an adjectival usage and could be strongly, although not conclusively, argued that Jesus' reference here was to a Christian. "Every branch in Me" would then be a good translation. If it modified the bearing of fruit then it would be an adverbial usage and would be saying nothing about the branch's actual position, but rather it would be saying everything about the context of the bearing of fruit. A good translation of this sense would be "Every branch that does not bear fruit in Me." Both would be proper translations, given the Greek language used here.

Are there any contextual hints on which way to understand this prepositional phrase? Yes! The prepositional phrase, "in Me," is used six times in this chapter. In five of the six cases, it can only be adverbial (15:4(2x), 5, 6, 7). In each of these uses Jesus was supplying the context or sphere for the action that was being affirmed by the verb. This seems to lean us quite heavily towards seeing an adverbial use here in 15:2 as well, although not exclusively.

A conclusion regarding this branch must wait until 15:6, because after mentioning this fruitless branch here in 15:2, Christ did not pick him up again until 15:6. But preliminarily, this individual's vital connectedness to Christ is at least called into question.

To some people this sounds strange and abhorrent, the idea that there would be unconverted people tied to the body of Christ in such a way that they seem to be members of it, while not actually being a part. But, this must be understood within the context of the differences between the universal church and the local church.

## Theologically Speaking

The New Testament church must be understood first and foremost as a holy community. The phrase, holy community, refers to a community set apart by God for God. In other words, the church is made up entirely of believers. This group of people composed entirely of believers is described as the body of Christ. In 1 Corinthians 12:12-13 these facts were brought together by the apostle Paul,

> For even as the body is one and yet has many members, and all the members of the body, though they are many, are one body, so also is Christ. For by one Spirit we were all baptized into one body, whether Jews or Greeks, whether slaves or free, and we were all made to drink of one Spirit.

There are no unbelievers, non-Christians, within the ranks of the universal church of Jesus Christ.

However, to fully understand the New Testament church one must recognize that this universal or invisible church is manifested in visible churches. The New Testament recognizes that in these visible churches, unlike the invisible church, there may and many times exist a mixed multitude. Within the ranks of the visible church there may exist unbelievers. The New Testament affirms this in at least a couple of different ways.

First, the New Testament exhorts church congregations against the very real possibility of false profession (1 Cor. 5:9-13). One of the simplest statements regarding this fact was made by the apostle Paul, who, after laying out the problems and solutions for the disobedient Corinthian church throughout 2 Corinthians, ended his epistle with these words, "Test yourselves to see if you are in the faith; examine yourselves! Or do you not recognize this about yourselves, that Jesus Christ is in you–unless indeed you fail the test?" (13:5) This assumes that failure was a possibility, in spite of the fact that they appeared to be members of the body.

There is a second way that the reality of unbelievers being a part of the visible church was communicated by the New Testament. It records several examples of unbelievers infiltrating the gathering of God's people. Of course, Judas is the prime example of this. But, he is not the only one.

At the conclusion of Jesus' instruction in the Sermon on the Mount, He engaged in an extensive discussion of fruit being a telltale way of identifying those who were truly a part of the faith. He capped off His comments with these words,

> So then, you will know them by their fruits. Not everyone who says to Me, "Lord, Lord," will enter the kingdom of heaven; but he who does the will of My Father who is in heaven. Many will say to Me on that day, "Lord, Lord, did we not prophesy in Your name, and in Your name cast out demons, and in Your name perform many miracles?" And then I will declare to

them, "I never knew you; depart from Me, you who practice lawlessness" (Mt. 7:20-23).

Clearly individuals who identified themselves as doing the things listed here would have been attached to a local body of believers.

Another example of this sort of manifestation took place in Acts 8 within the ministry of Philip the evangelist. The account of Philip's evangelistic labors among the Samaritan people included the manifestation of a false profession by a man named Simon. Simon, who had been a recognized magician of some significance in that region (8:9-11), seemed to have made a confession of Jesus Christ in response to the gospel preaching of Philip, along with many of the others who at one time followed Simon, followed by his baptism (8:4-8, 12-13).

However, Simon's response of amazement to Philip's miracles was only compounded when he witnessed the bestowing of the Holy Spirit on the Samaritan disciples by Peter, who had come down to Samaria to validate their conversions (8:13-17). Captivated by what he saw, Simon made a request to purchase the power Peter seemed to possess, which was met by not only a rebuke, but a call to repentance and a warning of spiritual condemnation (8:18-23). His lack of conversion came to the forefront in his response, "But Simon answered and said, 'Pray to the Lord for me yourselves, so that nothing of what you have said may come upon me'" (8:24).

The apostle John also provided an example of this very thing in his first epistle. While writing to the body which he was addressing, John felt the need to warn them about a group of individuals, false teachers, who were attempting to pervert the teachings sanctioned by him. His warning stated,

> Children, it is the last hour; and just as you heard that antichrist is coming, even now many antichrists have arisen; from this we know that it is the last hour. They went out from us, but they were not really of us; for if they had been of us, they would have remained with us; but they went out, in order that it might be shown that they all are not of us (1 Jn. 2:18-19).

These illustrations demonstrate the fact that it cannot be biblically denied that there is a possibility of unsaved individuals being a part of the local gathering of believers. While the church must seek to keep its membership pure, this will not be the unequivocal reality of the local church in this age. As such, before moving on to the second branch and its fruitfulness and thus its authenticity, the church must pay heed to the warning of Jude,

> Beloved, while I was making every effort to write you about our common salvation, I felt the necessity to write to you appealing that you contend earnestly for the faith which was once for all delivered to the saints. For certain persons have crept in unnoticed, those who were long beforehand marked out for this condemnation, ungodly persons who turn the grace of our God into licentiousness and deny our only Master and Lord, Jesus Christ (vs. 3-4).

# 5
# The Fact of Fruitfulness in the Church

*. . . and every branch that bears fruit,*
*He prunes it, that it may bear more fruit.*
*John 15:2b*

I was excited as I sat outside of his office that afternoon, not knowing quite what to expect. I was a student in my second year of Bible college and my Greek professor, who I idolized, had agreed to disciple me. I would get his special attention and he would lead me into a greater life of spiritual maturity. I didn't know quite what to expect.

Well, what I got was an education on how to apply the word to the life of a believer and how to pastor people with humility rather than pride. One of the first texts to which Dr. Friesen took me was 2 Peter 1:5-8. After reading them together he asked me if the qualities contained in these verses were to be added one at a time, to which I agreed. He then demonstrated that they are in fact cyclical and will consistently need to be addressed in my life, over and over again. I was going to go through stages of growth, as were the people in my church, and if I were to pastor effectively I must understand this truth. Jesus affirmed this fact when He addressed the fruitful branches within the church.

Although the true church, the universal or invisible church, is comprised of only believers, this does not mean that every believer is at the same level of spiritual growth. While on earth, as part of a local church, believers are at various levels of spiritual fruitfulness. This is due to many things, not least of which is where they are in the process of spiritual adjustment carried on by God. Jesus referred to this as pruning as He discussed the fruitful branch.

## *The Fact of Fruitful Branches*

In discussing the fruitful branches, Jesus said, "Every branch that bears fruit, He prunes it, that it may bear more fruit" (15:2b). The branch that brings forth fruit is not left alone. The vinedresser "prunes it." The Greek term from which this idea was taken was the word *kathairo*. Its literal meaning was to "make clean." It was a word that came from a family of words that was used to communicate "physical, religious, and moral cleanness or purity." The verb that Jesus used spoke to the purging or making of something clean in a religious sense. A very rare use of this term was to "clean away superfluous wood," that is, to prune. Jesus' use of this term to communicate the concept of pruning was very purposeful and strategic.

Pruning was a very important part of the vinedresser's work. If proper growth of the vine was to be maintained, then parts of the vine, which were unnecessarily absorbing the needed nutrients, had to be removed. Therefore, dead branches which were still being needlessly fed by the trunk of the vine had to be cut off so that the nutrients would not be wasted. The implications of this fact relative to the interpretation of 15:6 will be apparent.

Also, unnecessary foliage had to be pruned off of the healthy branches, so that live branches could continue to effectively grow, but now at an even greater rate and capacity. An experienced and skilled vinedresser was not satisfied with growth. Growth to him simply meant the potential for more growth, and he responded to growth by taking his pruning shears and cutting away, the unnecessary foliage, such that the healthy branch could "bear more fruit."

This act on the part of the vinedresser is not only telling for its purpose, but it is telling because of its factual reality. This action that Jesus attributed to the vinedresser, the Father, establishes a reality regarding the Christian experience that all believers must grasp and understand, if they are to navigate the ever-shifting nature of the Christian experience. There are levels of fruitfulness in believers. The fruit of the branch leads to more fruit through the actions of the vinedresser. This communicates the fact that the earthly Christian experience is one of progression, not completion.

The focus of Christ, however, in these words was to set forth God's, the vinedresser's, response to a healthy, growing branch, that is, the Christian. His response was not to celebrate the growth, but to dig in even harder to see more growth in that person's life. He prunes the believer's life, seeking to remove those realities that would be a hindrance to their growth. All true Christians possess things in our lives that hinder the fruit producing life surging in us from the vine, Christ, from having its fullest effect.

A portion of that hindrance is due to sin. This is the most obvious issue that hinders spiritual fruitfulness and to which is easily admitted. Peter understood this, evidenced by his exhortation to believers in 1 Peter 2:1-3, "Therefore, putting aside all malice and all guile and hypocrisy and envy and all slander, like newborn babes, long for the pure milk of the word, that by it you may grow in respect to salvation, if you have tasted the kindness of the Lord." Here the actions of the vinedresser, pruning or removing, is exhorted of believers.

Another portion or percentage of the hindrance to spiritual growth that resides in all believers comes from the reality of spiritual ignorance. God has given His Word to believers so that they might know certain realities, realities which are important to their growth and maturity in the Lord. Ignorance on their part is one of the ways that their growth in grace is not all that it should be and could be.

This was why the apostle Paul throughout his epistles gave instruction to the church so that they would not be ignorant of certain matters. So, for example, in addressing the Corinthians' failure to properly understand the basis of true spirituality, Paul began with these words, "Now concerning spiritual gifts, brethren, I do not want you to be unaware" (1 Cor. 12:1; cf. Rom. 11:25; 1 Cor. 10:1; 1 Thess. 4:13). The famous words of Hosea 4:6, "My people are destroyed for lack of knowledge," are even applicable to New Testament saints.

But these two are not the most devastating hindrances to our spiritual vitality. Both sin and ignorance are obvious issues that can be seen in believers themselves and would be readily admitted by saints about themselves. But the third hindrance lives in many believers who would never own it in their lives, and its existence can often escape the notice of others. This might be defined as spiritual slothfulness.

Many a true believer does not attain to what could be attained in their lives, because, quite frankly, they are sluggards when it comes to the matter of their spiritual maturity. They only want just enough spirituality. They want just enough Bible instruction. They want just enough service. They want just enough growth. Enough to just pass fruit inspection, to be left alone by the church leadership and other believers, but not enough to truly excel in the Christian life before God.

This very reality was part of the problem that the author of Hebrews sought to address with the people to whom he wrote. As he gave them instruction, he came to a point of hesitancy in his instruction and gave the following admonition;

> Concerning him we have much to say, and it is hard to explain, since you have become dull of hearing. For though by this time you ought to be teachers, you have need again for someone to teach you the elementary principles of the oracles of God, and you have come to need milk and not solid food. For everyone who partakes only of milk is not accustomed to the word of righteousness, for he is a babe. But solid food is for the mature, who because of practice have their senses

trained to discern good and evil (5:11-14).

Is it any wonder then, that the author began the very next chapter with a call to cast off their lethargy and halfheartedness, and to instead press on? He stated, "Therefore leaving the elementary teaching about the Christ, let us press on to maturity, not laying again a foundation of repentance from dead works and of faith toward God" (6:1).

## *The Response to Fruitful Branches*

Here is where many in the pews and the pulpits around America are satisfied to have attained. But be sure, God will not allow spiritual sloth, spiritual ignorance, or sinfulness to keep Him from getting what He wants out of the genuine saint, which is spiritual fruitfulness. After all, He has the pruning shears.

Now believers do not like this. In fact, they will do all in their power to avoid it. They will complain about it, because pruning hurts. Notice, in the text, that the pruning was not identified as taking place because of disobedience. The pruning took place because of obedience. It was the very signs of life, fruitfulness, in the branch that made the vinedresser work even more feverishly.

Anyone who honestly evaluates their lives as a Christian or the lives of other believers they know, will have to admit an important truth. One of the greatest hindrances to believers' spiritual growth is their hatred, bad disposition, complaining, and basic bad feelings toward God's pruning of their lives.

## THE FACT OF FRUITFULNESS IN THE CHURCH

They want to know why He is pruning. Why things are so difficult. Why things are going so bad for them. Why they seem to face these trials and tribulations. They face them because they are growing. If they are operating in good conscience before their Savior, they can be assured that those difficulties they are facing are Him working on them, attempting to perfect in them the work He has started in them.

After all, God plainly indicates in Philippians, "For it is God who is at work in you, both to will and to work for His good pleasure" (2:13). Is this not what Paul was reminding the Romans of when he wrote to them in 5:3-4, "And not only this, but we also exult in our tribulations, knowing that tribulation brings about perseverance; and perseverance, proven character; and proven character, hope"?

Now, this is not to say that the only pruning God uses to produce spiritual maturity, that is, fruitfulness in believers, is trials and difficulties. He uses the teaching and ministry of elders (Eph. 4:11-13). He uses the faithful implementation of the one another actions identified in the New Testament, practiced believer to believer (Eph. 4:15-16). He uses the weekly stimulation provided by other believers in the context of the corporate gathering (Heb. 10:23-25). He uses their own consistent incorporation of the Word of God into their lives (Jam. 1:21-22; 1 Pet. 2:1-3). He uses the spiritual power of Christ accessed through volitional intensity (Eph. 1:17-21; 2 Pet. 1:5-11).

Here are just some of the things God uses in believers' lives to move them to greater fruitfulness through pruning. This is the reality of the Christian life. This is that for which Christians signed up. This is the mark of authentic Christianity.

Now some deny the suffering aspects of this process and tell the church that God wants them healthy, wealthy, and wise. But from God's Word, God wants them pruned. And when they grow, He will prune them back. And when they grow some more, He will prune them back again; until the day that their final pruning happens and He takes them to be with Himself.

John 15:1-2 gives the foundation of growth in the believer's life. Growth does not happen independently of the vine. When a branch is cut off from the vine it does not grow, it cannot grow. Therefore, it is only in being properly connected to the vine that proper growth can take place, because the vine is the source of the life and nutrients that produce growth. It is also important to notice that even the producer of the growth is not the branch, but the vinedresser, who is God. He is the one who takes responsibility for growth.

A vinedresser is the person who guides and manages the growth of the vine. So too is God the guide and director of growth in the believer's life (cf. Phil. 2:12-13). Any good vinedresser makes sure that the plant, for which He is caring, has the proper nutrients and fertilizer, as well as the proper amounts of water and sunshine. He must also take into account the growth of the individual parts of the plant, and make the necessary adjustments to the plant regarding its growth, that is pruning. This is the context of fruitfulness.

## The Fact of Fruitfulness in the Church

In these verses, Jesus has established bearing fruit as a critical aspect of what truly attached branches produce. Further consideration of what this looks like will be brought forth in the following chapters.

# 6
# Biblical Sketches of Spiritual Fruitfulness

*And other seeds fell into the good soil*
*and as they grew up and increased,*
*they yielded a crop and produced thirty,*
*sixty, and a hundredfold.*
Mark 4:8

Up until this point in examining John 15, Jesus has interjected the concept of fruitfulness into His depiction of Himself as the vine and His Father, the Lord God, as the vinedresser. The reality of fruitfulness, however, goes beyond just this lengthy metaphor that appears within this passage. It is a biblically important principle taught and affirmed throughout the pages of the New Testament.

## *Spiritual Fruitfulness in the Ministry of John*

The first appearance of this concept within the New Testament occurred through the ministry of John the Baptist. John's ministry was introduced in the opening chapters of all the gospels. In Luke 3, after giving the timing of John's ministry in 3:1-6, Luke recorded the following facts,

> He therefore began saying to the multitudes who were going out to be baptized by him, "You brood of vipers, who warned you to flee from the wrath to come? Therefore bring forth fruits in keeping with repentance, and do not begin to say to yourselves, 'We have Abraham for our father,' for I say to you that God is able from these stones to raise up children to Abraham. And also the axe is already laid at the root of the trees; every tree therefore that does not bear good fruit is cut down and thrown into the fire" (3:7-9).

Here the idea of fruitfulness is used in the context of the call for sinners to turn from their sin and to embrace John's message of repentance, a message which will be carried forth by Christ Himself. Notice the following realities regarding fruitfulness from its first appearance. First, fruitfulness was separated from repentance. In other words, to bring forth fruit, was not the same as to repent, but rather these were two separate realities altogether.

Second, the order or the relationship between these two realties was that repentance led to fruit bearing not vice versa. This, of course, meant that repentance was spiritually primary in the relationship between them.

Third, the fruit was not determined by the repenter, but was the direct consequence of repentance. In other words, the fruit matched repentance, because of what repentance was, just as a rose matches a rose plant.

Fourth, the presence of good fruit, or its absence, demonstrated whether the axe and fire would be executed against that person. Fifth, the fruit was the manifestation of righteousness in the context of life (Lk. 3:10-14).

## Spiritual Fruitfulness in the Teaching of Jesus

This idea of fruitfulness demonstrated itself in the teachings of Jesus, as well. It first appeared at the conclusion of His Sermon on the Mount in Matthew 7, some of whose sayings would be paralleled in Luke 6.

### In the Conclusion of the Sermon on the Mount

Its context was in the exposing of false teachers. His concluding remarks properly summarize what He said in 7:15-18, "Every tree that does not bear good fruit is cut down and thrown into the fire. So then, you will know them by their fruits" (7:19-20).

The point of Jesus was that fruit identified the nature of the person's spiritual life, not that it determined it. What determined the nature of a person's spiritual life was the entering of the narrow gate and walking the narrow way described earlier in 7:13-14. Because of the existence of spiritual life in a person, the fruit was a consequence, which meant that, "A good tree cannot produce bad fruit, nor can a bad tree produce good fruit" (7:18).

These principles were applied to individuals who were not false teachers in Luke 6:43-45, thus showing their applicability not just to false teachers, but to the broader religious community as well.

## In the Parable of the Soils

Besides Jesus' teaching on fruitfulness found in John 15, probably the next most important explanation of it in His instruction occurred in the context of the parable of the sower. As one might expect, the connections between John 15 and this parable are not just on the surface. The idea of bearing fruit in this context was taken from two Greek terms, one communicating the idea of bear and the other fruit, which were brought together to form a single compound word, which was used in the gospel of Mark in Mark 4:20.

In this passage, Jesus offered His disciples the correct interpretation of the Parable of the Sower, where Jesus was recorded making the following concluding statement, "And those are the ones on whom seed was sown on the good soil; and they hear the word and accept it, and bear fruit, thirty, sixty, and a hundredfold."

The parable itself was communicated at the beginning of Mark 4, where Jesus combined a series of analogies into the following visual picture,

> Listen to this! Behold, the sower went out to sow; and it came about that as he was sowing, some seed fell beside the road, and the birds came and ate it up. And

other seed fell on the rocky ground where it did not have much soil; and immediately it sprang up because it had no depth of soil. And after the sun had risen, it was scorched; and because it had no root, it withered away. And other seed fell among the thorns, and the thorns came up and choked it, and it yielded no crop. And other seeds fell into the good soil and as they grew up and increased, they yielded a crop and produced thirty, sixty, and a hundredfold (4:3-8).

When the interpretation of this parable was given to the disciples in private in Mark 4:13-20, Jesus laid out the proper understanding of its meaning. His point was that the person doing the sowing was actually not sowing seed, but rather, he was sowing "the word," which immediately places these matters into the context of spiritual development in the lives of people. As such, each of the four soils represented a person.

In considering these four soils or rather souls, that is, people, Jesus definitively separated the first three from the final soil (soul). Only in the case of the final soil was the designation "good" used. None of the other soils bore that designation. This was key contextually as to why of all the four soils, only the final one produced the fruit that the sower intended in his carrying out of the act of sowing.

This adjective, "good," separated and distinguished the soil from the other soils identified in this story. The Greeks had more than one word for good. The term for good which was used here had a wide range of meaning and usage in the literature of Paul's day. In modern America, our tendency is to look at the concept of good in the Bible as moral all the time. While this term could refer to a moral goodness, it did so because, in the Scriptures, there developed a link between the divine and that which was good. What took place with the concept of good, biblically speaking, was that good could only be determined by that which aligned itself with the will and order of God.

However, the literal meaning of the term used by Mark to communicate what Jesus was describing in this parable referred to the concept of healthy, beautiful, attractive, or usable. This was clearly the meaning of good here in this parable. The soil was healthy soil, usable soil, soil that could properly produce that which was sown in it. This described its meaning in the parable itself, when Jesus used good to describe the soil in 4:8.

However, in the interpretation of the parable offered by Jesus, good was being used to describe a human heart (cp. Mt. 13:19 and Mk. 4:15) or soul that was capable of bearing the spiritual fruit of that which was sown in it, the Word. Thus, this distinguished the final soil from the previous three. It alone was capable of producing the type of fruit that the Word would produce, because it was good soil, that is, a good soul.

Again, keep in mind the reality that good must be defined both biblically and contextually. This is no more important than here in Jesus' interpretation in which He applied good to a soul. The world looks at human beings as having good souls. This is the basic worldly position, socially, politically, economically, and so on. But this position is quite different than what the Bible actually teaches. Christians believe that humanity is evil and his soul is corrupted by his evil nature. Ephesians 2:1-3 clearly states this case. Thus, for truly biblically thinking people, a good human soul is a soul properly aligned with God and His will, a soul regenerated and reoriented to God.

To fail to recognize a distinction between this final soil and the soils that precede it, is to fail to recognize the language used by Christ. He Himself made a distinction between the soils. He Himself defined the fourth soil in completely different terms than He did the others. He wanted His listeners to conclude that all the soils were not the same and the fourth soil was existentially different that the previous three.

Grasping these truths helps understand why the first three soils bear no fruit whatsoever. These soils, or souls, were characterized by Jesus as unresponsive to the Word of God. In the case of the first soul, there was no attempt to understand, thus, failure to understand is evident (Mk. 4:15). In reference to the second soul, there was a joyous reception that faded as quickly as it came (4:16-17). The third soul witnessed a cool calculation on false scales that counted what could be gained in this life as more important than what could be gained in the life to come (4:18-19).

But it was not just the nature of the fourth soul that led to its fruit bearing. Because of its nature, this individual responded in a certain manner to the communication of the Word. Jesus did not just define the soil, the human heart, by this adjective, but He went on and further described it with the following clause, "and they hear the word and accept it." The first half of this statement was true of all the soils, they all heard the Word. This was not unique to this fourth soil. What was unique, however, was the reality communicated in the statement, "and accept it."

The Greek word *paradechomai*, which has been translated "accept," carried two different ideas depending on whether it referred to a person or an object. Here an object was being referred to, the "word," specifically, so it meant to "acknowledge or accept something as true, or to admit something." What is implied from this meaning is that something so acknowledged or admitted to would be believed to be true and responded or acted upon (Ac. 16:21; 22:18).

Take for example the negative use of this idea in Paul's warning to Timothy in 1 Timothy 5:19, "Do not receive an accusation against an elder except on the basis of two or three witnesses." Why was this so important? Because Paul expected that true accusations would be acted on, as is clearly indicated in the following verse, "Those who continue in sin, rebuke in the presence of all, so that the rest also may be fearful of sinning" (5:20). So, the idea of this term was hearing something, acknowledging the truthfulness of it, and receiving it to oneself in such a fashion as to act on it.

This presents a sharp contrast with the other three soils. Does this not answer, the why behind these other soils? Why was there no response at all in one of the soils? Why did the response that did happen among the other previous two soils only evidence temporary or temporal efficacy? The problem was presented by Jesus in this interpretation not in the hearing of the ear, for they all heard what was said, according to His interpretation. But rather the central problem within these other soils was the failure to embrace the Word, to accept it for themselves, and then to act on it. Although the second soil was said to "receive" the Word with joy, it became clear that there was no acting upon it, thus their temporary nature.

So, this fourth soil represented the person who gets the meaning of the Word of God and its implications for their lives, and in turn lives it out. This further evidences that this fourth soil had the hand of God at work in their lives, this was why they got it. Paul makes this clear in 1 Corinthians 2:14-15, "But a natural man does not accept the things of the Spirit of God; for they are foolishness to him, and he cannot understand them, because they are spiritually appraised. But he who is spiritual appraises all things, yet he himself is appraised by no man." This connects the concept of the soul being "good," as a result of God's working in them, and thus being able to "accept" the Word.

The result of these facts is that they "bear fruit." As already noted, this phraseology links Jesus' statement in Mark 4 to His statement in John 15. It was Jesus' standard position that the truly converted, those branches who more than just appeared to be attached, but were actually attached, would manifest such a fact by bearing fruit. The fruit being discussed is the same in both passages, it is the product which is commensurate with the plant that brings it forth.

## *Spiritual Fruitfulness in the New Testament Letters*

This can be clearly seen in another passage in which this compound word can be used in both good and bad circumstances, which highlights that which was doing the producing was the point and not so much the fruit. In Romans 7 the apostle Paul was laying out the consequences of being united with Christ, which required a freeing from the Law. An early conclusion in this lengthy argument appeared in 7:4-5, where this term was used twice, "Therefore, my brethren, you also were made to die to the Law through the body of Christ, that you might be joined to another, to Him who was raised from the dead, that we might bear fruit for God. For while we were in the flesh, the sinful passions, which were aroused by the Law, were at work in the members of our body to bear fruit for death."

Now, what is clear from this passage is that the idea of bearing fruit was not inherently good or righteous in and of itself. The bearing of fruit is a necessary consequence to being alive. This is not a surprise since back in Romans 6, Paul used the term "outcome" twice, once to describe the result of slavery to sin, which was death (6:21) and once to describe the result of slavery to God, which was eternal life (6:22). The words are quite different, "outcome" and "bear fruit," but the point is similar. There is a consequence to the spiritual bent of a person's life. Both those who are the Lord's and those who are not manifest something, either life or death, as Romans 7 indicates, or righteousness or lawlessness, as Romans 6 indicates.

The fruit, then, produced by the godly, is wonderfully described in contexts in which this terminology is used in the good sense. This fruit is a gospel fruit, a fruit manifested by this word of truth. This is the case because Paul described the gospel in Colossians 1:6 as follows, "Which has come to you, just as in all the world also it is constantly bearing fruit and increasing, even as it has been doing in you also since the day you heard of it and understood the grace of God in truth."

But not only is it a gospel fruit, more specifically it is a fruit that can be described as good works. Paul indicated this, again in Colossians 1, as he went on to describe what motivated his prayer life for them. He prayed that they might "be filled with the knowledge of His will in all spiritual wisdom and understanding, so that you may walk in a manner worthy of the Lord, to please Him in all respects, bearing fruit in every good work and increasing in the knowledge of God"(Col. 1:9b-10).

These are just some of the examples of the fact that this fruit is described in various ways throughout the New Testament. In Ephesians 5:9 Paul wrote, "For the fruit of the light consists in all goodness and righteousness and truth." Philippians 1:11 described the believer as having been filled with the fruit of righteousness which comes through Jesus Christ. The author of Hebrews talked about discipline in this fashion, "All discipline for the moment seems not to be joyful, but sorrowful; yet to those who have been trained by it, afterwards it yields the peaceful fruit of righteousness" (12:11). James 3:18 reads as follows, "And the seed whose fruit is righteousness is sown in peace by those who make peace."

This righteousness was that to which Jesus was referring in His interpretation of the parable of the sower. However, what is important to recognize here is that the fruit bearing Jesus was describing differed within the final soil. This realization takes us back to one of the key points made in John 15:1-2. Not because we need to know that we will all bear fruit at various levels, although such is true, but even more so that we would see that the comparison between believers is found not between the four types of soil, but rather within the final soil itself.

In other words, the first three soils represent the unconverted, those who had rejected Christ, and only the final soil represented Jesus' true follower. Within this group is where the difference, between believers, lies. The branch that bore no fruit, could be any or all of the first three soils of Mark 4. The fourth soul and the fruitful branch were two different ways of representing the same person, the converted, maturing believer; they are fruit bearers, bringing forth righteousness, justice, all the fruit of the Holy Spirit.

The natural question that arises out of this consideration is, how does a person become the growing branch that is pruned, rather than the fruitless branch that is disposed of? Jesus moves to describe where the disciples stand in this process, as He issued a call to fruitfulness to them.

# 7
# The Prerequisite of Fruitfulness

*You are already clean because of the word*
*which I have spoken to you.*
*John 15:3*

We have already established the fact that behind Jesus' statements within this text was the reality of Judas. He was the unspoken subject of the dark side of what Jesus was saying in and through this parable. While Jesus will spend more time on the fruitful branch, one can only know such a branch fully when they see him against the backdrop of the fruitless branch. One of the clearest ties to Judas takes place as Jesus laid out why fruit was even possible within the life of those to whom He was specifically addressing this statement, the eleven disciples who remained after the departure of Judas. Jesus will take the disciples' minds backwards to move them forward.

When it comes to the matter of fruitfulness, as described in John 15, it will become clear that the disciples of Christ had no option in this process. This was something that happened through a proper connection to the vine. But the disciples were to play a part. Jesus addressed what their part was to be in the next four verses. In these verses, He communicated the basis of fruitfulness (15:3), the means of fruitfulness (15:4, 5), and the lack of fruitfulness (15:6).

If fruitfulness was going to take place, it demanded something, first and foremost, a real or actual relationship with the vine. Jesus addressed this in the first half of 15:3.

## *A Proper or Real Relationship with Christ*

Jesus made the statement, "You are already clean" (15:3a). The term "clean" was the Greek word *katharos*. This term was part of the family of terms that was used to communicate pruning in the previous verse. There the word was *kathairo*. Both terms sound similar, because they come from the same root word. *Kathairo* is the verb and *katharos* is the adjective of the family. *Katharos*, as was the case with *kathairo*, therefore, also basically meant clean, pure, or to make such.

As noted already, this family of terms spoke to the issue of making clean or purging. So, both terms essentially dealt with "physical, religious, and moral cleanness or purity." What was Jesus' sense here in verse three and what are the implications for what He has said that God does to growing branches in verse two? This term actually is the key to unlocking this entire passage, because this word is a reference to an event from an earlier context in the Upper Room Discourse.

Jesus was saying that the disciples were in a state of being pruned. The ongoing pruning that God effects in the life of the believer as testified to in 15:2 was essentially an extension of the forensic pruning that took place at salvation. God had and was pruning them in order to accrue greater amounts of growth from them. This brings up the issue of Judas, however. Was he included in this statement made in 15:3? Based on Jesus' statement in John 13:6-11, he was not. But the disciples did not know that.

John 13:6-11 demonstrated this. There Jesus was giving instruction on humility. He demonstrated the greatest show of humility by washing the feet of the disciples. Here the Teacher and Lord washed the feet of the disciples, how much more should they respond in like manner to each other and express their love for one another through humble service (13:13-17)?

While washing the disciples' feet, Jesus was prohibited by Peter from washing his feet. Jesus, however, made it clear that such a washing was necessary, for it was to be a testimony to Peter being His (13:8). Peter then made the brash statement that he wanted Jesus to take the dirty water that had been used to wash the other disciples' feet and to give him a bath in it. Christ's response to this request, made by Peter to try to save face before the Lord, was more than profound, it was theologically definitive.

In answering Peter, Jesus indicated that once "completely clean" one only needed to wash their feet. This spoke of the ultimate forgiveness which came from Christ, which after salvation came, only needed to be augmented by confession of and subsequent purification from daily sin. In this verse Jesus made the following statement, ". . . and you are clean, but not all of you" (13:10). This is a statement of exclusion of the one betraying Him (13:11). These verses provide the verbal link between chapter thirteen and chapter fifteen.

The same word "clean" used in 15:3, which was the root of the word "prune" in 15:2, was the same word found on the lips of Jesus for "clean" in chapter thirteen. His usage of "clean" in John 13 clearly excluded Judas, as the usage in John 15 must as well. The fact that Judas was excluded is also affirmed in 13:18-19. However, up to this point in the narrative, the disciples were still believing that Judas was included as indicated by John 13:29-30. So, when these statements are taken in light of the defection of Judas, they are properly understood as a statement of the identification of true believers in contrast to those who, like Judas, are false believers and thus do not produce fruit in Christ.

When the disciples in the future eventually looked back on Jesus' words about the vine and the branches, they would know that Judas was not clean; and, therefore, he was not one of the branches that bore fruit, although he seemed like he did, and although he seemed like he was a branch, when in actuality he was not. Although he preached and worked miracles with the rest of the disciples, although he was so trusted that he kept the group's money purse, yet he knew not the Savior as his own. The implications of this are played out in 15:6.

Jesus here, then, indicated that the disciples were clean in a moral and forensic sense. It is the experience of this forensic relationship that makes a person the second branch identified in 15:2.

THE PREREQUISITE OF FRUITFULNESS

## *The Cause of Such a Relationship*

In the second half of the verse Jesus communicated how they got to be in such a state. Jesus said, "because of the word which I have spoken to you" (15:3b). What was the word that was spoken by Christ that produced this forensic cleansing?

Throughout John's gospel the response to Jesus' words, sayings, or teachings determined the destiny of the hearers. The Scriptures and the word of Christ were equated with each other in 2:22, and both were responded to with belief. In 4:50-53, believing in Jesus' word of healing resulted in the actual healing of the nobleman's son.

The most significant type of word from Christ was that which led to life in a spiritual sense. Jesus made claim of this in John 5:24 which said, "Truly, truly, I say to you, he who hears My word, and believes Him who sent Me, has eternal life, and does not come into judgment, but has passed out of death into life."

This reality was experienced by the Samaritans, who after hearing from the woman who met Jesus at the well, went out to see this stranger themselves. And after listening to Him John recorded this, "And many more believed because of His word; and they were saying to the woman, 'It is no longer because of what you said that we believe, for we have heard for ourselves and know that this One is indeed the Savior of the world'" (4:41-42).

But Christ's word or words also separated and repelled just as they drew and compelled. No place is this more clearly illustrated than in the feeding of the 5,000 in John 6.

After Jesus had fed the 5,000 plus, He departed to the other side of the sea after praying. When the multitudes, who had eaten the previous day, found out He had left their area, they followed Him and sought Him not for how they might receive eternal life, but so they could eat breakfast (vv. 26-27). The people denied this, of course, but Christ validated as much through a series of dialogues in which He affirmed that if they were really concerned about life eternal they would eat His body, since He was the true bread which came down out of heaven (6:28-47).

The exchange climaxed in 6:48-51, in which Jesus not only explicitly made the connection between Himself and the Manna from the Old Testament, indicating that He was the new bread, but went one step further and indicated that He needed to be eaten. The response of the Jews to this was that they "began to argue with one another, saying, 'How can this man give us His flesh to eat?'" (6:52).

Rather than backing up, Jesus turned on the heat in 6:53-58 indicating that not only did they need to eat His flesh, but they also needed to drink His blood, that is, fully embrace Him by faith. This was the only way for them to live, in a spiritual sense.

The reaction of some to this was telling. 6:60 says, "Many therefore of His disciples, when they heard this said, 'This is a difficult statement; who can listen to it?'" The word "statement" or "saying" could also be translated "word." Now notice how Jesus responded to this reaction of His followers in 6:61-65,

## The Prerequisite of Fruitfulness

> But Jesus, conscious that His disciples grumbled at this, said to them, "Does this cause you to stumble? What then if you should behold the Son of Man ascending where He was before? It is the Spirit who gives life; the flesh profits nothing; the words that I have spoken to you are spirit and are life. But there are some of you who do not believe." For Jesus knew from the beginning who they were who did not believe, and who it was that would betray Him. And He was saying, "For this reason I have said to you, that no one can come to Me, unless it has been granted him from the Father."

Now notice the response of these supposed followers of Christ in 6:66, "As a result of this, many of His disciples withdrew, and were not walking with Him anymore." Jesus used this to confront the twelve in 6:67-71,

> Jesus said therefore to the twelve, "You do not want to go away also, do you?" Simon Peter answered Him, "Lord, to whom shall we go? You have words of eternal life. And we have believed and have come to know that You are the Holy One of God." Jesus answered them, "Did I Myself not choose you, the twelve, and yet one of you is a devil?" Now He meant Judas the son of Simon Iscariot, for he, one of the twelve, was going to betray Him.

Jesus' point was, were they going to go away or were they going to remain and abide with Him? The disciples recognized there was nowhere else to go. They may not have understood what Jesus was saying, but whatever it was, they knew that they had to believe it and act upon it. By the way, notice, through this critical dialogue on true salvation through embracing Him and His word, the contrast with Judas was made by the author.

This passage clearly indicated that Christ's word, in other words, His teaching, both draws and confirms, as well as separates and repels. The mark of truly being one of His is remaining within the confines of His word. Jesus claimed this in John 8:31-32, when John recorded the following interaction, "Jesus therefore was saying to those Jews who had believed Him, 'If you abide in My word, then you are truly disciples of Mine; and you shall know the truth, and the truth shall make you free.'"

Jesus was not saying that one works for their salvation by remaining in His word, for that would be salvation by works. Rather the validation of a person's true possession of that salvation is demonstrated through their remaining in the context, boundaries, and sphere of Christ's word.

No wonder that one of the signs of not being a true follower of Christ is Christ's word not playing this high point in one's life. Jesus said in 8:37, "I know that you are Abraham's offspring; yet you seek to kill Me, because My word has no place in you." These Jesus calls sons of the devil in 8:44. So, Jesus' words created divisions (10:19). On which side of the division one came down, validated who they truly were.

The disciples had come down on the right side of Christ's word, by having embraced His message through faith; therefore, it could be said of them that they were clean. This

## The Prerequisite of Fruitfulness

spoke of that forensic or positional cleaning experienced in justification, through the means of Christ's message.

Fruitfulness begins with a right relationship with Jesus Christ. Just as Jesus stated in Matthew 7:16-18, "You will know them by their fruits. Grapes are not gathered from thorn bushes, nor figs from thistles, are they? Even so, every good tree bears good fruit; but the bad tree bears bad fruit. A good tree cannot produce bad fruit, nor can a bad tree produce good fruit." They had been positionally pruned, so now they were eligible to be progressively pruned in an ongoing fashion. Believers call that type of pruning sanctification.

# 8
# The Roadmap to Fruitfulness

*Abide in Me, and I in you.*
*As the branch cannot bear fruit of itself,*
*unless it abides in the vine, so neither can you,*
*unless you abide in Me. I am the vine,*
*you are the branches; he who abides in Me,*
*and I in him, he bears much fruit;*
*for apart from Me you can do nothing.*
*John 15:4-5*

God is the sovereign controller of the spiritual growth of those who are part of His church. We have already established this fact. Does this mean that man plays no role in the process of growth? Is spiritual growth simply a monergistic reality, something that God does alone and we are only along for the ride? Or is it more than that? From the picture painted by Jesus in John 15, it becomes clear that man does play a role in his spiritual growth, although not a determinative one, but rather a responsive one. Many years after Jesus gave this parable, Paul would make the following declaration,

> So then, my beloved, just as you have always obeyed, not as in my presence only, but now much more in my absence, work out your salvation with fear and trembling; for it is God who is at work in you, both to will and to work for His good pleasure (Phil. 2:12-13).

Having laid out the role of the Father and Son in the matter of fruitfulness in the church, as well as the human participants to life of the vine, Jesus will now bring these two ideas together to layout the disciples' active involvement in the process.

What was required of them? What part must man play? In looking at fruitfulness from the vantage point of the disciple in 15:4-5, Jesus will state its source, its inevitability, and man's inability. In looking at 15:4-5 one will notice that they say the exact same thing, just differently. 15:5 says positively what 15:4 says negatively. Because of this, combining them brings their message out in a clearer fashion.

## *The Source of Fruitfulness*

Jesus began both of these verses by indicating the source of fruitfulness. In verse four He said, "Abide in Me, and I in you" (15:4a) and in verse five He said, "I am the vine, you are the branches" (15:5a). The first statement communicated His thought without the accompanying imagery, while the second statement maintained that imagery. When you put these two ideas together, what Jesus was communicating to the disciples was that they were to abide in Him and such an abiding was reflected or imaged in the manner or way that a branch was connected to the vine of which it was a part. The relationship was to be as intimate, integral, and immediate as the relationship between a vine and its branches.

The word "abide" was translated from the Greek word *meinate*, which is a derivative of the verb *meno*. It had two basic meanings "stay or remain," on the one hand, and "await," on the other. The first meaning had a number of nuances or senses. Stay could mean to stand fast against opposition of some type, or stay in the sense of staying still, or stay in the sense of remaining or staying power. Probably the most dominant nuance was to stay or remain in a place. In this way, it could be used in the quite literal sense as in the case of John 1:38, "And Jesus turned, and beheld them following, and said to them, 'What do you seek?' And they said to Him, 'Rabbi (which translated means Teacher), where are You staying?'" or John 2:12, "After this He went down to Capernaum, He and His mother, and His brothers, and His disciples; and there they stayed a few days."

However, this term began to take on a very significant meaning when this literal nuance was used figuratively for remaining in a particular sphere. John used this figurative sense extensively throughout all his letters. John talked about: 1) the wrath of God staying or remaining on those who reject Christ (3:36); 2) those who don't believe Christ, not having the Father's word staying or remaining in them (5:38); 3) those, who as a result of eating Christ's flesh and drinking His blood, staying or remaining in Christ (6:56); 4) sins staying or remaining on persons who do not recognize their lostness before Him

(9:41); 5) those who believe in Him not staying or remaining in darkness (12:46); 6) the Father being in Christ in such a way that He stays or remains in Christ, so that what Christ says is of the Father's initiative; and 7) the Spirit staying and remaining with the believer, making Him unknowable to the world, since He will be in the believer (Jn. 14:16-19).

From all of these uses of the figurative sense of *meno*, one is left with the impression that this was not speaking of some type of mystical and esoteric experience. What Jesus was saying was very concrete. Abiding in Him was staying in the sphere or context of His will and His words which revealed it, and doing so even in the face of pressures that would normally move one to do otherwise. We would call it believing or trusting in Him. Such a reality both ushers one in and keeps one throughout the process (Jn. 6:54, 56; 8:31; 15:9-11). This is the mark of the true disciple of Christ.

By the way, this is exactly the opposite of the response of the second soil in the parable of the sower. Jesus noted,

> And in a similar way these are the ones on whom seed was sown on the rocky places, who, when they hear the word, immediately receive it with joy; and they have no firm root in themselves, but are only temporary; then, when affliction or persecution arises because of the word, immediately they fall away (Mk. 4:16-17).

The individual's response to the Bible is a telltale indicator of a person's positioning with Jesus Christ.

John 6 witnessed to this through those who did not abide, but rather, when the commitment and the understanding got to a high or difficult level, they split. Their lack of unwavering and unflinching belief in Christ manifested itself. This exhortation by Christ makes perfect sense in light of Him giving these instructions in the context of Judas' defection.

Judas did not remain; he did not continue in belief. Judas and the disciples who left in John 6 did not lose their salvation, they manifested the fact that they never had it. They abandoned physically what they had never ultimately committed to spiritually through faith. No wonder the shock and urgency of Paul's words to the Galatians in 3:1-5,

> You foolish Galatians, who has bewitched you, before whose eyes Jesus Christ was publicly portrayed as crucified? This is the only thing I want to find out from you: did you receive the Spirit by the works of the Law, or by hearing with faith? Are you so foolish? Having begun by the Spirit, are you now being perfected by the flesh? Did you suffer so many things in vain-if indeed it was in vain? Does He then, who provides you with the Spirit and works miracles among you, do it by the works of the Law, or by hearing with faith?

Paul was genuinely concerned, so much so that he warned them in 5:2-7 in terms quite Pauline in nature yet strikingly familiar to Jesus' words in John 15. He wrote in 5:2-7,

> Behold I, Paul, say to you that if you receive circumcision, Christ will be of no benefit to you. And I testify again to every man who receives circumcision, that he is under obligation to keep the whole Law. You have been severed from Christ, you who are seeking to be justified by law; you have fallen from grace. For we through the Spirit, by faith, are waiting for the hope of righteousness. For in Christ Jesus neither circumcision nor uncircumcision means anything, but faith working through love. You were running well; who hindered you from obeying the truth?

This truth was what led John to pronounce over those who had removed themselves from the church and the truth of Christ, "They went out from us, but they were not really of us; for if they had been of us, they would have remained with us; but they went out, in order that it might be shown that they all are not of us" (1 Jn. 2:19).

So, when Christ commanded them to abide in Him and that the reciprocal would take place, He abiding in them, He was calling them to a protracted or persevering faith or belief evidenced by remaining with Christ and obeying His Word through all pressures and temptations to do otherwise.

## *The Inevitability of Fruitfulness*

If such takes place, that the disciple lives his life by consistent, albeit imperfect faithfulness, something will inevitably occur. It was to this point that Jesus then turned: the inevitability of fruitfulness. Again, both verses four and five give the same idea but with different words. 15:4 described the byproduct of abiding in these terms, "the branch cannot bear fruit of itself, unless it abides in the vine" (15:4b). In the following verse, He framed His idea in this manner, "he who abides in Me, and I in him, he bears much fruit" (15:5b).

Again, as with the opening statement of both verses, so too here we see that these two statements make both a figurative statement and a statement devoid of the figure. Both statements deal with the inevitability of fruit bearing from a positive and negative perspective. The first statement indicated that bearing fruit was impossible without abiding, and the second statement indicated that bearing fruit was possible by abiding. These statements need not even be proven for they were plainly the case. A branch could not sprout fruit if it was unattached to the vine. Such is impossible. The only feasible way for a branch to bear fruit is through its connection to the vine.

This reality is compounded more exponentially in reference to Christ; because, unlike just a regular grapevine, He is the very source of the life that shows forth itself in the fruit spoken of here. A literal grapevine has life as a derivative of the fact that it is created by God. Its life is contingent or dependent on something else, and it is manifested in other living things, even other grapevines. However, the life that spawns the fruit of the Christ vine cannot be attained from any other source than Jesus Himself. For example, in the immediate context of this statement we read, "Jesus said to him, 'I am the way, and the truth, and the life; no one comes to the Father, but through Me" (14:6).

But even more to the point regarding the issue of life are the words of Jesus Christ while in a debate regarding His divinity. To the Jews that were doubting Him, Jesus made the following statement, "For just as the Father has life in Himself, even so He gave to the Son also to have life in Himself" (Jn. 5:26). What this means, then, is that being properly connected to Him results in the bringing forth of "much fruit." This does not occur by happenstance; it is inevitable. A rose plant will bring forth a rose, if it is in fact alive.

If there is nothing wrong with the branch and nothing wrong with the vine, then fruit will be an inevitable byproduct of the union between the two. Although the fruit appears on the branches of the vine, it appears because of the connection that is maintained between the two. This is Jesus' point. The union itself will produce the growth, not the action of the branch. The fruit is something that springs from the relationship. While the human source of fruitfulness may be in the Christian remaining committed in faith to Christ and His word, it is not the ultimate source of that fruitfulness. The ultimate source is the relationship from which fruit will spring necessarily, as grapes necessarily spring forth from living grapevines.

The unified voice of Scripture is in support of this fact. Jesus' disciples embraced this doctrine and communicated such to those who followed them. The broader New Testament Scriptures assume that all truly healthy Christians produce the fruit of righteousness, the manifestation of the eternal life conveyed from the vine to the branches. Romans 6:17-18 stated, "But thanks be to God that though you were slaves of sin, you became obedient from the heart to that form of teaching to which you were committed, and having been freed from sin, you became slaves of righteousness."

1 John 3:10 said, "By this the children of God and the children of the devil are obvious: anyone who does not practice righteousness is not of God, nor the one who does not love his brother." It is for this reason that when the believer's bearing forth of fruit becomes scant the Bible exhorts him to examine himself. Paul told the Corinthians, "Test yourselves to see if you are in the faith; examine yourselves! Or do you not recognize this about yourselves, that Jesus Christ is in you–unless indeed you fail the test" (2 Cor. 13:5).

Jesus affirmed this point in ending these verses with a statement of man's inability in fruitfulness.

## *Man's Inability in Fruitfulness*

Jesus closed these verses with the following statements, "so neither can you, unless you abide in Me" (15:4c) and "for apart from Me you can do nothing" (15:5c). Fruit bearing was not a matter of the efforts of the branch. Fruit bearing was a manifestation of the life that was resident in the vine. Jesus indicated to the disciples that they were completely dependent upon Him for the life that they were to live.

Modern man does not like this of course. He likes to stick out his chest at his accomplishments. He likes to consider himself something, when he is nothing. Before God, man stands completely helpless, and if not for the moving of God, he would perish.

Again, this is a manifestation of what took place in salvation. Within the hymns of the church, there is a hymn that goes something like this: "I was sinking deep in sin, far from the peaceful shore, very deeply stained within, sinking to rise no more; but the master of the sea heard my despairing cry, from the waters lifted me, now safe am I." The hymn does not completely convey the teaching of the Scriptures. It was not that sinners were sinking, but rather according to Scripture they had sunken and were floating on the top of the sea, dead, a cold corpse.

Ephesians 2:1 says, "And you were dead in your trespasses and sins." Oh, they were alive, but only in a physical sense. They were a monster, a zombie if you will. They were part of the walking dead. Alive physically, but dead spiritually. Their spiritual death meant, according to Romans 3:11, that they did not understand nor did they seek after God. Salvation came to them because of a divine act, in which God scooped up their dead corpse and again, as He had done with Adam, breathed the breath of life into their decaying spiritual nostrils. Wholly of God.

At salvation, they had nothing but their sin to offer to God. God moved in grace, mercy, and love to regenerate a dead man. The Christian life is the same. It is not accomplished through your efforts. You are rather responding to God's work in you. What else do you think Paul meant when he said in Philippians 2:12-13, "Work out your salvation with fear and trembling; for it is God who is at work in you, both to will and to work for His good pleasure"? You respond to the work of God in your life. When God convicts you of sin, how do you react? When God moves you through His Word to begin changing your pattern of life, either by stopping certain practices or starting others, how do you react? Does God even move you in these ways? Do you desire such a move of God in your life? It is God at work in you, both to will and to work, the Bible says.

The life of the vine will demonstrate itself or prove itself to be so in the fruitfulness of the branch. If it does not, we must call the life of the vine into question. However, since the vine is Christ, the problem must lay not in the vine in this case, but wholly the branch instead.

# 9
# The Judas Branch:
# The Reason for Fruitlessness

*If anyone does not abide in Me . . .*
*John 15:6a*

In His opening words to the eleven apostles in John 15, Jesus has established the reality that fruitfulness springs forth from the true believer's life as grapes spring forth from a branch properly connected to a vine. The presence of fruit gives witness to the reality of the conversion of that professing believer. However, throughout the New Testament there exists another reality, a reality that Jesus will affirm next in John 15. That reality is the fact of false profession.

Now many within the church do not want to admit that such a thing happens and that it is given witness to through the reality of fruitfulness or its lack, but such cannot be denied. A couple of verses from the Corinthian letters demonstrate the truthfulness of this fact. First, that such a reality exists was brought to the surface in Paul's words in 1 Corinthians 5 as Paul dealt with the church's unwillingness to deal with individuals within their ranks who were living in open rebellion against God.

One such individual was identified in this chapter, and in dealing with them, Paul not only instructed them to apply church discipline to him in 5:1-8, but also reminded them of his past instructions which should have guided their present behavior towards him, but had not up to this point. He penned the following;

> I wrote you in my letter not to associate with immoral people; I did not at all mean with the immoral people of this world, or with the covetous and swindlers, or with idolaters; for then you would have to go out of the world. But actually, I wrote to you not to associate with any so-called brother if he should be an immoral person, or covetous, or an idolater, or a reviler, or a drunkard, or a swindler-not even to eat with such a one. For what have I to do with judging outsiders? Do you not judge those who are within the church? But those who are outside, God judges. Remove the wicked man from among yourselves (5:9-13).

The so-called brother was the individual who had attached himself to the local church, who claimed to be a believer, but chose to live a godless life. Such individuals must be responded to in a certain fashion by the local church because of its commitment to biblical purity (5:6-8).

But this is not just a matter for the church in its character as a corporate body to consider, it is also a matter for the individual believer to swallow hard and consider as well. As you know, the church of Corinth had taken up the counsel of some false apostles who were denying Paul's authority and affirming their own (2 Cor. 11). Paul, on a number of occasions throughout these letters, found himself having to defend his apostleship. As he drew 2 Corinthians to a close, he warned those within their ranks, who were continuing to affirm this, that while they may have felt safe within the group, he was coming and when he came, he would come with the full authority and power of the risen Lord who commissioned him as an apostle (13:1-4).

He then issued a warning, a warning that called into question the sinful disposition that these certain ones were expressing. Paul stated, "Test yourselves to see if you are in the faith; examine yourselves! Or do you not recognize this about yourselves, that Jesus Christ is in you-unless indeed you fail the test?" (13:5). Rejecting apostolic authority was no light matter and such might be evidence that one was not truly converted. After all, John said in 1 John 1:3, "What we have seen and heard we proclaim to you also, that you also may have fellowship with us; and indeed our fellowship is with the Father, and with His Son Jesus Christ."

What the apostles taught on the issue of the reality of false profession in the church and the fruitfulness or lack thereof within the believer being a witness to such, finds its New Testament archetype within the words of Christ in John 15. Having dealt with the basis and means of fruitfulness in 15:3-5, Jesus will now conclude His call to fruitfulness with an affirmation regarding the lack of fruitfulness.

The fruitless branch mentioned earlier in 15:2 again becomes the focus of Jesus' attention. He will give the reason for fruitlessness, the reaction to fruitlessness, and the result of the reaction to fruitlessness. Regarding the reason for fruitlessness, Jesus said, "If anyone does not abide in Me" (15:6a).

Jesus shifted from the more specific and direct "you" of the previous verses, to the more general "anyone." This clearly introduced the idea of the hypothetical into His description of these branches. He was no longer addressing the disciples directly, for He had already identified them as being "clean" according to 15:3, or justified as indicated in John 13. Thus, here He began dealing with individuals who would fall outside of that particular realm.

Although these words contextually within the Upper Room Discourse apply directly to Judas, Jesus also knew that the apostles would start a movement called the church that would have great extension beyond themselves. This is plainly stated in His great words in Matthew 16, which demonstrate this fact,

> And Jesus answered and said to him, "Blessed are you, Simon Barjona, because flesh and blood did not reveal this to you, but My Father who is in heaven. And I also say to you that you are Peter, and upon this rock I will build My church; and the gates of Hades shall not overpower it. I will give you the keys of the kingdom of heaven; and whatever you shall bind on earth shall be bound in heaven, and whatever you shall loose on earth shall be loosed in heaven" (16:17-19).

## THE JUDAS BRANCH – THE REASON FOR FRUITLESSNESS

These words are famous and well known. However, even within the context of Jesus' words in the Upper Room there is an assumption of this very thing. In Jesus' prayer for these eleven men, He made note of the following,

> As Thou didst send Me into the world, I also have sent them into the world. And for their sakes I sanctify Myself, that they themselves also may be sanctified in truth. I do not ask in behalf of these alone, but for those also who believe in Me through their word; that they may all be one; even as Thou, Father, art in Me, and I in Thee, that they also may be in Us; that the world may believe that Thou didst send Me (John 17:18-21).

The eleven disciples and the one who would eventually replace Judas, making twelve again, would begin a movement, or rather entity, called the church. The church would have to deal with the matter of hangers on like Judas, who confessed to be saved, but knew not Christ, that is, experienced nothing of the Master. The use of "anyone" broadened the scope of Jesus' words and pushed the meaning of the text towards the future church they would plant.

The problem with the fruitless branch identified in 15:2 and elaborated upon here in 15:6 was that it had failed to remain in Christ, it had failed to continue on in dependent belief, faith, and trust in the Savior. It had manifested that it was not clean, which was the basis of abiding and its consequence of bringing forth fruit, addressed by Christ earlier.

The inevitable link between abiding and fruitfulness was here affirmed yet again, even in this negative circumstance. You see, Jesus did not say "If anyone does not bear fruit," but rather, "If anyone does not abide in Me." He could say this because He had already established the fact that those who abide bear fruit, just as those branches of a vine that are alive bring forth fruit. Thus, a failure to abide meant a failure to produce fruit, because fruit was the inevitable consequence of abiding.

These concepts, abiding and bearing fruit, were therefore interchangeable, one being used in 15:2 of the false branch and the other being used in 15:6 of the same branch. It can therefore be drawn from this that the failure to produce fruit was a manifestation that the branch that seemed to be integrally connected was actually a branch by itself, as 15:4 warned. Such disconnected branches cannot bear fruit.

By way of illustration, it is seen within the teaching of Jesus Christ the recognition of the dual realities of the converted and the unconverted existing within the bounds of His corporate people. In Matthew 7 Jesus indicated that false teachers are manifested by their fruit, or rather their lack thereof. He then went on to say beginning in 7:21,

> Not everyone who says to Me, "Lord, Lord," will enter the kingdom of heaven; but he who does the will of My Father who is in heaven. Many will say to Me on that day, "Lord, Lord, did we not prophesy in Your name, and in Your name cast out demons, and in Your name perform many miracles?" And then I will declare to

them, "I never knew you; depart from Me, you who practice lawlessness" (7:21-23).

You will notice here that Jesus communicated that there would be a group of the unconverted, though operating within the context of God's people, prophesying in Jesus' name, casting out demons, and performing miracles, who would not actually be a part of His people; they would not be truly attached to Him, which Jesus affirmed by speaking about their lack of fruit.

We see the parallels between that situation and the situation described by Christ in John 15. In both situations, we have individuals that hang on to the corporate entity as if they were attached, but in all actuality, they were not attached at all. The connection or relationship was a hoax, a fabrication. For a time, it looked like they were really connected, really were a part. It looked like they were really enjoying the life of the vine or the benefits of the Lord's community. Their true nature will eventually manifest itself, here on earth or in judgment before Christ.

The parable of the sower of the seed gives a pointed statement as to what could have happened with these individuals. Jesus indicated in Matthew 13:20-21, "And the one on whom seed was sown on the rocky places, this is the man who hears the word, and immediately receives it with joy; (but wait, Jesus says) yet he has no firm root in himself, but is only temporary, and when affliction or persecution arises because of the word, immediately he falls away" (parenthesis added). By the way "word" is the same Greek term as "word" in 15:3. Why did this branch not bear fruit? "There was no firm root in" him.

Jesus next indicated what the reaction to such a situation would be.

## 10
## The Judas Branch:
## The Reaction to Fruitlessness and Its Result

*. . . he is thrown away as a branch, and dries up;
and they gather them, and cast them into the fire,
and they are burned.*
*John 15:6b, c*

     One of the key identifying characteristics of a local church is the reality of church discipline. Although many churches struggle with its implementation today, one is hard pressed to deny its importance to the church when it appears not only in the Old Testament, but the teachings of Jesus, and the instructions of the New Testament epistles. It is one of those spiritual characteristics that appears in all manifestations of the people of God on the earth.

     But discipline within the people of God should be seen as a reflection of God's own relationship with His people, not something His people do of their own origin. In concluding one of the several places that he discussed the matter of church discipline, Paul wrote these words, "For what have I to do with judging outsiders? Do you not judge those who are within the church? But those who are outside, God judges. Remove the wicked man from among yourselves" (1 Cor. 5:12-13).

This part of church life is a manifestation of the Lord's own role in purifying His church. Jesus indicated within this parable that the care of His church would be ultimately validated by Him in the end.

## *The Reaction to Fruitlessness*

This person "is thrown away as a branch" (15:6b). The phrase "thrown away" is a key phrase for properly identifying the identity of the fruitless branch. Its significance rests not so much in its apparent meaning, which would be tantamount to discarding something, but the significance of this phrase lies in its reference, or its usage in the teaching of Jesus. Earlier in John's gospel Jesus used this exact same phrase.

Like many of the other references from this chapter, chapter six is the source of the other appearance of this phrase. As noted earlier, chapter six was the story of the reaction of those who had attempted to make Jesus a bread king. Jesus confronted them over their ultimate physical desires, which they were masking under the guise of spirituality. These were the ancient counterparts to those who preach a prosperity gospel today and put it in the guise of something spiritual. Jesus made a statement of their unbelief in 6:36 when He said, "But I said to you, that you have seen Me, and yet do not believe." Although they were interacting with Christ, they did not truly believe in Him.

Jesus then began a series of statements regarding those who were truly His. In 6:37 He said, "All that the Father gives Me shall come to Me, and the one who comes to Me I will certainly not cast out." The final phrase of this verse was almost an exact duplicate of the phrase in 15:6. In 15:6 the phrase is *ballo exo* and in 6:37 the phrase is *ekballo exo*. *ekballo* is a derivative of *ballo*. The difference is not significant.

These two phrases while not identical have the same meaning. In fact, these phrases are many times translated in the same way, communicating their interchangeable character. This is obviously yet another strike against the fruitless branch being a believer. True believers, Jesus said, He "will certainly not cast out." Yet if this branch was a believer in John 15, Jesus would be doing the very thing that He said He would not do, which is casting them out.

So, this individual could not be a branch, but rather must be someone who looked as if they were connected, but were not actually in a vital relationship with the Savior. When does this throwing away occur?

## *The Result of the Reaction to Fruitlessness*

The removal of the branch from the corporate context in which it presumes itself to be, results in a certain series of four events taking place, "and dries up; and they gather them, and cast them into the fire, and they are burned" (15:6c). These four events can be divided into three snapshots or sequences regarding the fruitless branch.

The first sequence is the immediate outcome of the discarding of the branch. Jesus said that when the action of throwing away the branch takes place, the immediate result of that action is it "dries up." The true nature of the branch comes to the forefront. The life it seemed to possess was not truly life, but simply the appearance of life. Being in the context of life can make someone seem like they possess life when they really do not.

Do not miss what Jesus has just said here. The branch only "dries up" upon the casting out. What is the point? Until then, the branch, by implication, would have foliage, the rudimentary signs that it might be alive, but the factual matter of it actually being dead is witnessed to by its lack of fruit. Again, what we have here is yet another indicator of the fact that the individual that bore no fruit did seem to be a branch for a time, but its true nature was eventually manifested, as clearly was the case with Judas.

I had an interesting experience one day shortly after we had moved to Atlanta, Georgia, from Dallas, Texas, to pastor Berean Bible Baptist Church. As I was going into the basement of my house one morning, it looked like a light was on. I was the first person going into the basement, so I thought maybe one of the lights had been accidently left on overnight by the children. When I got downstairs no lights were on, but for the first time I realized that the windows in the basement were on the east side of the house and received the early morning light. It gave the impression that the basement lights were actually on, although they were actually turned off.

That is the way it was with Judas, the way it is with some religious people, and the way it is with some people who attend church. Their lives seem to emit light from a divine power source. The spiritual lights powered by the Holy Spirit seem to be turned on in their lives, when in fact their lives are simply lit spiritually speaking because of all the other actual spiritual lights all around them.

When my basement no longer receives the light of the day, when you go down there, unless you turn on a light source, it is pitch black. This is what Jesus was saying. When the branch is removed from the context of life, its lack of life will be clearly manifested, showing externally, what has always been true of it internally; it is marked by death, rather than by life.

The second sequence is comprised of two actions. Jesus said, "they gather them, and cast them in the fire." All these branches that fit into this category are bundled up. The gathering in of things was a common eschatological theme in the ministry of Christ. In the New Testament, the association between gathering and eschatology was made first by John the Baptist in Matthew 3:12, when he said, "And His winnowing fork is in His hand, and He will thoroughly clear His threshing floor; and He will gather His wheat into the barn, but He will burn up the chaff with unquenchable fire." From John's usage, three elements of this gathering are established.

First, the gathering is something that the Messiah does. Second, the gathering involves a separation between the good (wheat) and the evil (chaff). Third, the separation issues in a placement somewhere, either in a place for later retrieval, the barn, or a place for destruction, unquenchable fire. These three basic elements will manifest themselves when eschatological gathering is in mind. Probably the clearest example of this is found in a series of parables given by Christ in Matthew 13. An eschatological gathering appears in the second parable, the parable of the wheat and the tares.

The wheat of course were believers and the tares were the unconverted. The last verse of the parable said this, "Allow both to grow together until the harvest; and in the time of the harvest I will say to the reapers, 'First gather up the tares and bind them in bundles to burn them up; but gather the wheat into my barn'" (13:30). This is explained by Jesus in the following manner. He will issue the order to His angels to gather all the lawless ones, that is, all those who are not part of His true family, and they will be taken to judgment (13:41-42). On the other hand, the righteous, that is, the wheat, will be with the Father in His kingdom. This same concept is apparent in the parable of the dragnet given in 13:47-52.

So, this gathering that Jesus was speaking of here was to be a gathering with eschatological implications. The "they" who do it being angels dispatched by Christ Himself. The casting of them into the fire, is the eschatological judgment, that is the end times judgment of hell spoken of throughout the gospels.

The third sequence is obvious, then, "they are burned." While the meaning seems simple and straightforward to anyone who reads the text, the implications have driven many a commentator to offer a proposed interpretation to get around the implications that the branches that do not bear fruit will be destroyed in hell. In spite of the mounting evidence identified throughout this passage, some still hold that this unfruitful branch was actually a Christian and that this burning was simply a description of a believer losing their rewards. All that has come before, they argue, was a record of Jesus chastening the branch that does not grow properly. Many times, 1 Corinthians 3 is used to support this view of a loss of rewards. In that passage the hay, wood, and stubble of the ineffective believer is burned up, but his salvation is still intact.

The problem with such an interpretation, however, is that it just does not meet up to the exegetical realities of both of these texts. In 1 Corinthians 3:10-15 it is the person's works that are burned up. In John 15 it is not the works that are burned up at all, but rather it is the person himself. The Bible never talks about or infers that believers themselves could be burned up.

Jesus has concluded His identifying of the two possible types of individuals that identify themselves with the church. The first branch, the fruitless branch, was the religious and a lost person. Such an individual, like Judas, will eventually be exposed for his fraudulent religious life, either in this life or the life to come.

The second branch, the fruitful branch, was the truly converted person. They had genuinely responded to the word of God and continued to do so, resulting in the production of those spiritual qualities produced by Christ's work in them. They abide in Christ.

Given that abiding in Christ is such a central point to the matter of bringing forth the fruit that is being illustrated in this parable, how is abiding in Christ manifested in the Christian's life? Jesus will take up this issue next, looking first at abiding in Christ as obeying His word.

# 11
# The Fertilizer of Fruitfulness: Obedience to the Word

*If you abide in Me, and My words*
*abide in you, ask whatever you wish,*
*and it shall be done for you.*
*John 15:7*

In contemplating the words of the Psalmist in Psalm 1:3, "And he will be like a tree firmly planted by streams of water, which yields its fruit in its season, and its leaf does not wither; and in whatever he does, he prospers," Charles Spurgeon wrote, "But the man who delights in God's Word, being taught by it, bringeth forth patience in the time of suffering, faith in the day of trial, and holy joy in the hour of prosperity." We must be very careful to look for the right fruit upon our tree. Without rightly directing our affections and desires towards the Word, we will not fully experience the realities that grow forth from a person's connection with Christ.

Jesus told the disciples three important things by which true abiding would be defined in the life of the truly converted, those who are clean, as stated in 15:3. A person who was abiding would obey Christ's word (v. 7), glorify God (v. 8), and love Christ (vs. 9-11). Each of these has implications for the fruitful life that marks the true convert of Jesus Christ, which has been the focus of Christ's previous thoughts.

## *The Fruitful Believer is Marked by Obeying God's Word*

Jesus, in the concluding words to the parable of the vine, addresses the matter of how the believer effects abiding in Him. It begins with the Word of God, the only trustworthy source of all matters having to do with the beliefs and life of the believer.

For the disciple to abide in Christ, he will of necessity be practicing obedience to Christ's word. This was an implication drawn earlier in this book and the disciples being clean. However, Jesus did not leave it to implications, but rather in a straightforward manner, explicitly stated such to be the case in 15:7. He stated that such was the case and then gave one of the things that would result from such a commitment.

### Abiding as Obedience

Jesus began by stating, "If you abide in Me, and My words abide in you" (15:7a). The wording of this statement was very similar to the beginning of verses four and five. However, Jesus replaced the second half of the statement with something different, identifying instead a very important aspect to abiding in Him. Rather than abiding and producing fruit, which has been His point up to this stage of His argument, Jesus substituted in its place "and My words abide in you." This really served to direct the disciples toward what abiding in Christ included or how it was to be manifested. This is the assumption or premise of abiding. So, what does it mean for Christ's words to abide in a person?

Well, the concept of the Word of Christ abiding in a person is not unique to the New Testament, once its meaning is broadened to the Word of Christ being the Word of God Himself. The divine word abiding or remaining in a person is a concept that arose early within the biblical text. For example, it appeared in one of the most critical passages penned by Moses, which would eventually become a part of the great Shema of Israel. Right in the midst of what would serve as a part of Israel's prayer, that was repeated twice a day, appeared these words, "And these words, which I am commanding you today, shall be on your heart" (Deut. 6:6). Here the Lord commanded Israel through Moses to internalize God's Word. Why? So that they might teach it (6:7-9) and live in light of it (6:10-19).

The psalmist also spoke of this response to God's word among the righteous. When describing the true believer's response to God's Word in every verse of Psalm 119, one of the descriptions was as follows, "Thy word I have treasured in my heart, that I may not sin against Thee" (119:11). The emphasis on the heart in both of these texts, Deuteronomy 6:6 and Psalm 119:11, focus the believer upon the very core or center of his being, the focal point of his determination and decision. This is the execution of the believer's will. The godly man in

Proverbs knew this, for his father had given him the following instructions, "Then he taught me and said to me, 'Let your heart hold fast my words; Keep my commandments and live'" (4:4).

This reality appeared in the prophets as well. Jeremiah, although in a state of pity over what was taking place with him and the ministry to which he had been called, prayed to the Lord, reminding the Lord of certain things including "his faithfulness in bearing reproach, his love for His word, and his separation from evil men to stand alone (15:15-18)."[16] Regarding his love for His word, he wrote, "Thy words were found and I ate them, And Thy words became for me a joy and the delight of my heart; For I have been called by Thy name, O Lord God of hosts" (15:16). Again, the believer internalizing the Word of God was described.

So, believers in the Old Testament were commended to internalize God's Word. To consider this as simply Scripture memory would be to miss the point of the biblical authors. It referred to the study of and meditation upon God's Word, whereby it would become a part of who you were and as such would naturally begin to form and fabricate, that is, construct the believer's conduct.

To Jesus, who has obviously picked up on this idea in John 15, the problem with the Jews was to be found in their rejection of His Word. Take the incident in John 8. After warning those who had supposedly believed in Him to abide in His Word, things deteriorated to such a point that Jesus eventually said of them, "I know that you are Abraham's offspring; yet you seek to kill Me, because My word has no place in you" (8:37).

## THE FERTILIZER OF FRUITFULNESS – OBEDIENCE TO THE WORD

The internalizing of God's Word was commanded of the believer in the New Testament epistles. In sharing with the Colossians regarding living out the new life that became theirs when they came to know Christ, Paul gave them a series of exhortations that should define their lives. One of those exhortations had to do with God's Word, of which Paul noted, "Let the word of Christ richly dwell within you, with all wisdom teaching and admonishing one another with psalms and hymns and spiritual songs, singing with thankfulness in your hearts to God. And whatever you do in word or deed, do all in the name of the Lord Jesus, giving thanks through Him to God the Father" (3:16-17).

So, the abiding of Christ's word in the believer speaks to the believer's desire for and internalization of the Word of God, combined with the faithful belief and trust in that Word. Thus, one can hardly make a claim of abiding in Christ who does not remain consistent in his compliance with the Word of Christ. Well did the psalmist write in the first half of Psalm 1,

> How blessed is the man who does not walk in the counsel of the wicked, Nor stand in the path of sinners, Nor sit in the seat of scoffers! But his delight is in the law of the Lord, And in His law he meditates day and night. And he will be like a tree firmly planted by streams of water, Which yields its fruit in its season, And its leaf does not wither; And in whatever he does, he prospers (1:1-3).

Such a consistent act as this, Jesus indicated, would usher in a particular result.

## Results in Answered Prayer

When the believer lives in this fashion, Jesus promises them the following, "ask whatever you wish, and it shall be done for you" (15:7b). This verse, like others in this passage, has also been misunderstood and misinterpreted by many. Some take it as a blank check from God to answer in the affirmative any request made to Him in faith. All one would have to do is to believe that they have received it and it would be given unto them, no matter what it was. In essence, they were to simply speak it into existence.

This, however, misses the point of the passage within its given context. Why would Jesus, who has been talking about the believer living in faithful obedience to Christ evidenced by the bearing of fruit, which He will pick up again in the next verse, all of sudden begin addressing general, unrelated matters? Such does not fit this context. The verse actually has both a specific and a general meaning within this context.

The specific meaning is based on the context in which it appears. What is the "whatever" being referred to? Whatever has to do with the bearing forth of fruit in one's life as a true disciple. As you seek God regarding the bearing of fruit and you are faithfully adhering to His words, your requests will be answered in the affirmative. It is always Christ's will that His people bring forth fruit.

## THE FERTILIZER OF FRUITFULNESS – OBEDIENCE TO THE WORD

The general meaning has to do with prayer in general. The foundational reality of what Jesus is saying here is that the only prayers that He will answer are prayers that align with His will, not our will. The whole concept of speaking things into existence or getting whatever you claim by faith, assumes that the will of God is whatever we want. This however is as far from the truth regarding prayer as possible.

The promise voiced by Jesus here was given to the person who was completely saturated in Christ's words, that is, the Bible. Such a person will obviously pray in correspondence to Christ's will, which is revealed in His words. John clearly understood Christ's thought on this matter, for he himself stated this truth elsewhere when he wrote his own description of prayer in 1 John 5:14-15, a description which matched perfectly with Jesus' ideas, "And this is the confidence which we have before Him, that, if we ask anything according to His will, He hears us. And if we know that He hears us in whatever we ask, we know that we have the requests which we have asked from Him."

Christ only answers prayers that align with His will, which can only be known through His words. So, the first key to abiding is obedient fidelity to the words of Christ. This marks the general bent and purpose of the believer's life. One cannot claim to be abiding if such is not true of them. Those who do abide will have their prayers regarding their fruitfulness answered.

## 12
# The Fertilizer of Fruitfulness: Glorifying God & Loving Christ

*By this is My Father glorified, that you bear much fruit, and so prove to be My disciples. Just as the Father has loved Me, I have also loved you; abide in My love. If you keep My commandments, you will abide in My love; just as I have kept My Father's commandments and abide in His love. These things I have spoken to you, that My joy may be in you, and that your joy may be made full.*
*John 15:8-11*

There can be no remaining within the context of Christ, without the proper disposition to Christ. Jesus began His explanation of how true growth takes place within the body of Christ with the role of His Father and Himself in the entire matter. Jesus will close out with both of them.

## *The Fruitful Believer is Marked by Glorifying God*

Not only was obedience to God's word key, if one was going to abide as described by Christ in this passage, but also glorifying God was a centerpiece of this reality. Jesus will both state such and give an implication of such in 15:8.

## Bearing Fruit Glorifies God

Jesus said, "By this is My Father glorified, that you bear much fruit" (15:8a). Jesus in this statement reintroduced the Father, the vinedresser, back into the fruit bearing discussion, having left Him unmentioned since 15:2. It was noted in examining 15:4-5 that fruit bearing took place as a natural outgrowth of the relationship between the disciple and the Lord. But, something else was also clear there, which was the inability of the branch, that is the disciple, to produce the fruit that it was in fact manifesting. In speaking of spiritual consequences accomplished in the church, Paul made the following statement, "Now there are varieties of gifts, but the same Spirit. And there are varieties of ministries, and the same Lord. And there are varieties of effects, but the same God who works all things in all persons" (1 Cor. 12:4-6).

The one accomplishing this fruit bearing was the vinedresser Himself, who was the One ultimately responsible for the connection between the vine and the branch, the connection which produced the fruit. There is a certain response that God takes to the accomplishment of His work, He glorifies Himself. Although there are undoubtedly human agents involved in the processes of growth, their recognition was not what was important, but rather God's. He alone is worthy of praise and acknowledgment of fruit's production.

Again, in 1 Corinthians Paul noted, "What then is Apollos? And what is Paul? Servants through whom you believed, even as the Lord gave opportunity to each one. I planted, Apollos watered, but God was causing the growth. So then neither the one who plants nor the one who waters is anything, but God who causes the growth" (3:5-7). God's purpose for the believer bringing forth fruit is the glory of Himself. John described this idea of glory with the Greek term *dokazo*, which was related to the term upon which our English word doxology is based.

It was derived from a term that meant to think, admit, or claim. It spoke to a judgment or opinion made of someone, that is, to esteem or honor someone. When the word came into biblical usage in the translating of the Hebrew Old Testament into Greek, it developed the meaning of "to be heavy." The reason for this meaning was that because of one's weightiness they were esteemed or respected. In referring to God it spoke to His splendor, majesty, loftiness, and greatness.

Jesus' point here was as follows. The disciple who faithfully adheres to Christ's words will have his prayers regarding his spiritual growth answered, Christ's desire being his desire. When his prayers are answered he will find himself bearing much fruit. That fact validates or puts on display God's work as the vinedresser transferring back to God all splendor and majesty since that fruitfulness could only be accomplished by God Himself. So, in essence the believer glorifying God serves as both the motivation for his behavior and the result of his behavior.

## Bearing Fruit Results in Assurance

But there is a result for the believer as well. God was not the only one who benefitted from this process. Jesus said, "and so prove to be My disciples" (15:8b). Some translations say, "so be My disciples." In this statement, there is a mark of contingency to truly being one of Christ's. Given the context of the defection of one of their ranks, such contingency was to be expected. Remember, that Jesus was exposing in this passage the Judas branch, the branch that looks like it is attached to the vine, although it was not.

But what was Jesus saying here, since He had already declared them to be clean? Was He saying that somehow truly being disciples was earned through bearing fruit? That would be out of step with the rest of His own teaching as well as the other Scriptures which affirm that salvation is a gracious act, initiated and executed by God. So, what was the point?

Well, those who are truly disciples are already known by God and Christ, since they are omniscient. So their being known as disciples in this statement must be a human fact. What is the point here, then? Well, it is that as and only as a believer bears fruit does he and others receive full assurance of his truly possessing that which he professes to have. This was no different, in fact, from what Jesus had said earlier in Matthew 7:18-20, "A good tree cannot produce bad fruit, nor can a bad tree produce good fruit. Every tree that does not bear good fruit is cut down and thrown into the fire. So then, you will know them by their fruits."

On the other hand, a lack of bringing forth fruit as they ought would result in the conviction and discipline of God, because God will not have any of His own unhindered in their disobedience. God will not stand idly by while true believers resist His will and thus reduce the yield of the fruit. This is why the author of Hebrews wrote,

> And you have forgotten the exhortation which is addressed to you as sons, "My son, do not regard lightly the discipline of the Lord, Nor faint when you are reproved by Him; For those whom the Lord loves He disciplines, And He scourges every son whom He receives." It is for discipline that you endure; God deals with you as with sons; for what son is there whom his father does not discipline? But if you are without discipline, of which all have become partakers, then you are illegitimate children and not sons (Heb. 12:5-8).

There are only two options for true believers. Either they will bring forth more fruit through God's pruning, or they will be corrected through discipline to lead them to bringing forth more fruit. That is the lot of legitimate children. Either way, you will bring forth fruit.

## *The Fruitful Believer is Marked by Loving Christ*

Jesus now gave His third catalyst to the believer abiding. Not only must they obey Christ's words and glorify His Father, but they must also maintain a loving relationship with Him.

**LIFE IN THE VINE**

## Abiding as Love

In 15:9 Jesus established the connection between abiding and love. He first gave the basis of love and then related it to the disciples' relationship with Him.

*The Basis of Love*

The basis of love is found in the relationship between Christ and the Father. Jesus said, "Just as the Father has loved Me." Throughout Christ's life, He affirmed a special relationship between the Father and Himself. In John 3:35 He said, "The Father loves the Son, and has given all things into His hand." Again in 5:20, "For the Father loves the Son, and shows Him all things that He Himself is doing; and greater works than these will He show Him, that you may marvel." 10:17 said, "For this reason the Father loves Me, because I lay down My life that I may take it again."

This relationship extended across every aspect of Christ's life and ministry from Christ's words to Christ's works, from Christ's will to Christ's mission. His entire life and being was permeated and marked by the love of the Father. The love of the Father was the special care and disposition of kindness and priority towards the Son so that everything that was the Father's also belonged to the Son.

*Relating to Christ's Love*

This divine relationship marked by love is the one into which the believer is incorporated. As such, Jesus commended them in the following fashion, "abide in My love." As any good Son, Christ mimicked His Father. John 5:19 says, "Jesus therefore answered and was saying to them, 'Truly, truly, I say to you, the Son can do nothing of Himself, unless it is something He sees the Father doing; for whatever the Father does, these things the Son also does in like manner'" (cf. 5:30; 6:38; 8:28; 12:49; 14:10). It is no different regarding love, for Christ said, "I have also loved you." This same love that He received, He extended to the disciples. This special care and disposition of kindness and priority He received, He gave to them.

We get this sense so clearly in 13:1, "Now before the Feast of the Passover, Jesus knowing that His hour had come that He should depart out of this world to the Father, having loved His own who were in the world, He loved them to the end." Jesus appealed to them to therefore, "abide in My love," the love He had been expressing towards them. They were not to go outside of the love of Christ. How were they to do such? He answered this in the next verse.

## The Explanation of Abiding in Love

Jesus explained abiding in His love by telling the disciples how such was done, and then referring them to an example of it.

### *Its Meaning*

The means of their abiding is, "If you keep My commandments, you will abide in My love" (15:10a-b). The disciple would know for sure that he was remaining in the context of Christ's love, if he was consistently keeping Christ's commandments. This same affirmation was made in 13:34 and 14:15, 21, 23-24. It was in the set of verses in chapter fourteen that a key connection was made to explain the keeping of the commandments.

In 14:21 Christ appealed to the disciples to keep His commandments. Such would evidence their love and would lead to the love of the Father and the disclosure of Christ to them. Judas (not Iscariot) questioned how such could take place in 14:22. In 14:23-24 Jesus restated Himself but this time the wording was slightly changed. His "commandments" were adjusted to His "word" and "words."

Abiding in Christ's love was equal to abiding in His commandments, which was in turn equal to abiding in His word. To love Him was to obey Him, and to obey Him was to love Him.

*Its Example*

The ultimate example of this was Christ and the Father. Christ said, "just as I have kept My Father's commandments, and abide in His love" (15:10c-d). Christ tenaciously remained within the boundaries of the Father's will. He said that His very food was to do the Father's will in 4:34. More dear to Him was the Father's will than food itself. In 5:30 He said that He sought the Father's will.

Even when faced with the certainty of judicial separation from the Father on the cross, Christ's words were, "My Father, if it is possible, let this cup pass from Me; yet not as I will, but as Thou wilt" (Mt. 26:39). The disciples were to have the same tenacity in reference to the will of Christ as revealed in His words.

## The Result of Abiding in Love

Such behavior will have its benefits for the disciple. Jesus, in speaking to the disciples, said that He had communicated these things to them "that My joy may be in you, and that your joy may be made full" (15:11). Christian joy is that divinely given disposition and state in which the Christian lives and abides. It causes the believer to delight in Christ and His benefits and enables him to resist the influence of either positive or negative circumstances to determine his attitude.

This understanding of joy fits perfectly well into the context of John 15 where true joy for the disciple is found, not in the execution of his own will, but rather in the will of his Master, Christ.

# Conclusion

*So then, you will know them by their fruits.*
*Matthew 7:20*

Jesus has presented a profound picture of the Christian life, a life of fruitfulness. This fruitfulness comes from those who have a real relationship with Christ, who have been cleansed through having their sins forgiven upon accepting for themselves the finished work of Christ (15:3). This fruit referred to a life characterized by a vitality of Spirit produced qualities, which were defined and expressed by faithfulness in belief and conduct to Christ and His teachings, also known biblically as the fruit of the Spirit.

The responsibility of the believer in bringing forth this fruit is to persist in faithful belief in Christ's word and through that to foster a relationship of intimacy with the Savior (15:4-5). The fact of the believer maintaining such a relationship with Jesus Christ will definitively result in the bringing forth of spiritual fruit, because such fruit is a natural byproduct of that relationship, just as grapes come from being attached to branches, and not of the believer's efforts (15:4-5).

In contrast, complete fruitlessness is due to there only being an apparent relationship, rather than a real one (15:6). Such apparent relationships will be eventually judged and emphatically severed, resulting in the revealing of the true character of the branch and its final destruction in hell. The key element missing from this individual's life is the reality of abiding.

Jesus closed out his explanation of abiding by describing three key aspects or characteristics of it. A true believer abides in Christ by obeying Christ's word (15:7), by seeking to glorify God (15:8), and by loving Christ (15:9-11).

# APPENDIX A

## The Deeds of the Flesh (Galatians 5:19-21)
## A Life Devoid of the Spirit's Control

In the Upper Room Discourse, Jesus addressed the fact of the fruitless branch, the Judas branch. The true nature of this type of branch manifests itself in that it does not bear fruit, and therefore it is not connected to the true Vine. However, not only does the Judas branch bear no fruit, but a further look at the Scriptures indicates that it evidences something entirely different. In Galatians five Paul calls what it does the evidence or manifestation of "the deeds of the flesh."

Before investigating the life devoid of the Spirit's control, Paul presented his explanation of the Spirit controlled life. He examined its nature in 5:13-18. In these verses he presented the fact that the Spirit controlled life is a life of constant effort marked by selfless service produced from love and personal behavior that manifests continuous growth in the qualities and virtues produced by the Spirit. What do these qualities and virtues look like? What are they? In the second half of his explanation of the Spirit controlled life, the apostle

Paul examines the manifestation of the Spirit controlled life. In other words, what those qualities and virtues are.

In Galatians 5:13-18, the Spirit controlled life is set in contrast to what the flesh wants to do in the believer's life. Paul warns against allowing Christian freedom to become a jumping off point for the flesh. He also indicates that the flesh desires to actualize sin in the believer's life, and to this regard it positions itself against the Spirit. The Spirit controlled life is the only type of life that can resist the flesh in its attempt to manifest itself in the believer's life.

Paul carries these two great contrasts into the next section, further delineating just how much at variance these two opposing means of living life have with each other. In examining the manifestation of the Spirit controlled life, Paul investigates not just the positive, but also the negative as well, the life with and without the control of the Spirit. By doing this he presents a thorough examination of the manifestation of the Spirit controlled life. In 5:19-21 Paul looks at the life that is devoid of the Spirit's control, and in 5:22-23 he educates the Galatians on the life that manifests the Spirit's control. The concluding verses of this section, 5:24-26, summarize and give the ramifications of what the apostle has been trying to get the Galatians to understand regarding the outcome of the gospel that he preaches. So, Paul begins with the negative side, the lack of Spirit control and its ramifications for a person's life.

The life devoid of the Spirit's control is a horrific one indeed. The flesh in action produces certain deeds. Paul examines these deeds in 5:19-21, by looking at the nature of the flesh's deeds, the deeds produced by the flesh, and the consequences of those deeds.

## *The Nature of the Flesh's Deeds*

Paul starts out with a statement as to the nature of the flesh's deeds. He writes, "Now the deeds of the flesh are evident" (5:19a). The focus of Paul's statement is upon the term "evident." In the Greek text it is at the very head of the clause, indicating that Paul is placing emphasis upon it. It is derived from the Greek word *phaneros*. This word was used to express or describe something that was "open, manifest, or conspicuous." This was used in the political process of Paul's day to describe voting by a show of hands in distinction to voting by ballot. The vote by show of hands would be publically known and therefore plainly recognizable to all. Therefore, it could be used to describe something as being "well-known." A good rendering in the context would be notorious.

"Deeds of the flesh" signify those acts that are produced by the flesh. The noun "deeds" is translated from a basic term used to communicate any type of work or result of effort of any sort. It had a neutral meaning and therefore drew its significance or sense from the context in which it appeared. In the Bible it is primarily used in an ethical sense to communicate either morally upright behavior or morally reprehensible behavior. Here it is obviously the latter that Paul is focused upon since the deeds are coming forth from the flesh.

The deeds of the flesh are one step beyond the desires of the flesh that were referenced in 5:16 and the opportunity for the flesh in 5:13. The three ideas are connected in the following manner. The flesh is seeking an opportunity to have its desires actualized in the believer's life by certain sinful acts which the apostle Paul here calls deeds. The deeds or acts that the flesh wants to produce, the apostle labels as "notorious." These acts are not mysteries or secrets, but rather they are publically known. While the extent or form of wickedness might change, the nature of it is always obvious and known to man, no matter how much he tries to deny such things as being evil. Paul gives a list of the types of acts that the flesh tries to produce.

## *The Deeds Produced by the Flesh*

From 5:19 to 5:21 Paul gives a list of fifteen of the flesh's deeds. Paul does not intend for this to be an exhaustive list because at the end of it he writes, "and things like these." In other words, the deeds of the flesh include all these things plus any other deed that is like the ones he has listed. There exists a multiplicity of ways in which the flesh seeks satisfaction. While it is difficult to know whether Paul purposefully placed these in groups, the list does reveal a certain order to it. Included in the lists were sexual, religious, relational, and substance oriented sins. We will look at this list in that order.

### Sexually Oriented Sins

The sexually oriented sins are listed first and are as follows: "immorality, impurity, sensuality" (5:19b). It is interesting that Paul begins the list with these items. One of the strongest passions in the human heart is the desire for both emotional and physical intimacy. God placed it there, but the fall of man perverted it. Paul here gives three types of sexually oriented sins that the flesh produces.

The first deed that the apostle lists is "immorality" which is derived from the Greek term *porneia*. Obviously, this is the term from which developed our English term pornography. However, *porneia* goes beyond what most people label as pornography, which are pictures of unclothed people. *Porneia* stands for any type of extramarital physical intimacy, whether it be adultery, fornication, homosexuality, incest, or any type of illicit union outside the marriage bond.

The second deed is "impurity," which is translated from the Greek term *akatharsia*. This term referred to something being impure or dirty, whether it be physically, ceremonially, or morally. For example, a sore or wound that was infected and therefore oozing with pus would be considered unclean. It is the opposite of being cleansed and therefore pure. This term is often linked with *porneia* and when such takes place has a somewhat broader meaning than the latter. So, this term would refer to not just illicit unions, but any act or activity that was sexual in nature that might fall short of a union of some type.

The third deed listed is "sensuality," which is from the Greek noun *aselgeia*. This word had a general meaning of excess or overindulgence, in other words, to take things to the extreme. William Barclay defined it as "a love of sin so reckless and so audacious that a man has ceased to care what God or man thinks of his actions." This is sin without boundaries. In Paul's day the term was quite often used to focus upon sexual sin, as it does here in our text. Most of the uses in the New Testament have such a meaning. This term speaks, not so much to the acts as does *porneia*, or the grossness and dirtiness of the acts as does *akatharsia*, but rather to "unrestrained willfulness" and wantonness in the sexual arena.

These first three deeds of the flesh have a particularly defiling nature on the person themselves. Of these types of sin Paul writes in 1 Corinthians 6:18, "Flee immorality. Every other sin that a man commits is outside the body, but the immoral man sins against his own body." There is a peculiar, defiling effect not just in the act itself and not just on the other person, but also on the body itself.

## Religiously Oriented Sins

Paul now moves to the next set of sins, that of religiously oriented sins. Paul lists two of them, "idolatry, sorcery" (5:20). The act of idolatry is translated from *eidololatria*. This word is only used in the New Testament. It is derived from the Greek term *eidolon*, which referred to the image of a god or the god that the image symbolized. Therefore, *eidololatria* refers to the worship of the false god represented by the idol. This particular sin is attached to other acts in the New Testament besides just the overt veneration of the idol. Both the participation with celebrations that take place in the idol temple that are not explicitly worship oriented and greediness are considered idolatry by the apostle Paul (1 Cor. 10:14-22; Col. 3:5).

The second term, "sorcery," is from the Greek term *pharmakeia*. Of course, this term sounds like our English word pharmacy and pharmaceutical, of which it is the basis. The term itself stood for the dispensing of drugs for medical reasons. However, two particularly negative uses for this term developed because of its association with drugs. First, it could be used to refer to the poisoning of people, since just as there are good drugs, there are obviously lethal ones as well. The second developed usage was the use of drugs in sorcery and witchcraft. Certain drugs in Paul's day, just as in ours, could be used to induce altered states of consciousness. These would be used in cultic and occult ceremonies and practices. This led to this term being associated with black magic and the black arts, which is a perversion of true religion.

## Relationally Oriented Sins

The flesh also manifests itself in relationships. This is the most extensive elaboration of the sins produced by the flesh of all the four areas that Paul identifies. Could it be that we tend to sin in this area more than any other? Paul lists eight different sins in this area, "enmities, strife, jealousy, outbursts of anger, disputes, dissensions, factions, envying" (5:20-21).

The first sin listed is "enmities," *echthra* in the Greek. This word means "hostility" and "hatred." This refers to both a disposition, as well as the actual conflict itself that led to the disposition.

The next sin in the list is "strife," which translates *eris*. This term refers to discord, wrangling, or contention. It is the outbreak of hostility, the arguing and fighting between parties that evidences an evil, wicked attitude and disposition.

The third sin is "jealousy," coming from *dzelos*. This term is given both a positive and a negative meaning in the Scriptures. The positive meaning is "zeal" or "enthusiasm" which refers to a "deep concern for or devotion to someone or something." The negative meaning of jealousy, which is used here, refers to envy or resentment. This is an attitude that begrudges someone else.

The following words "outbursts of anger," are translated from one Greek term, *thumos*. This word also had both a positive and a negative meaning. It could refer either to courage or to a very intense anger marked by fits or outbursts. It is not the settled indignation of God and in some cases what we know as righteous wrath, but rather it is an outburst of passion, a "passionate outburst of hostile feelings."

The fifth sin comes from the Greek word *eritheia* and means "disputes." The first occurrence of the term in the Greek language that we have on record is in Aristotle's writings in which this term referred to a politician seeking support through self-promotion so as to gain office for his own benefit. The word derives from a term that means to "work for wages." This positive meaning later develops into the idea of doing something for one's own personal profit. In other words, to be self-seeking, ambitious for one's own self, or selfishly devoted to one's own interests. This is the meaning here in 5:20.

The sixth relational sin is "dissensions," translated from *dichostasia*. In the culture of Paul's day this term stood for dissensions or seditions, usually of a political nature. The idea of this term is that of the divisions produced by disagreements in general. Such divisions are a work of the flesh.

## A LIFE DEVOID OF THE SPIRIT'S CONTROL

The next sin listed is "factions," coming from *hairesis* in the Greek. This term, *hairesis*, is the word from which we derive our English term heresy. The word has three uses, "a division or group based upon different doctrinal opinions and/or loyalties, in other words a sect," "the content of teaching that is not true, that is false doctrine or heresy," or "a division of people into different and opposing sets, in other words division or separate group." Given the focus of self-seeking ambition and divisions in the previous two terms, the third use of this term is being employed here, focusing upon factions created probably by religious beliefs, as was evident in Corinth.

The eighth sin identified by the apostle is "envying," which is translated from the term *phthonos*. This term is very close in meaning to jealousy, which was used earlier in the list. The nuances are a little different, however. Jealousy, as used earlier, carries the idea of wanting to be in the same condition as another person. Envying, on the other hand, carries the idea of the ill-will and malice that would lead one to want to deprive another of what he has.

With this, Paul concludes his list of eight relationally oriented sins. These are actions that destroy relationships and the unity that the Spirit has produced. People oftentimes live in these sins for years thinking that God is still working in their lives and answering their prayers, when He has in fact completely shut off heaven from them. One only need to read Matthew 5:21-26 and Luke 17:1-10 to see the seriousness of these sins.

## Substance Oriented Sins

The last sins that Paul gives in his list are sins associated with substance abuse, "drunkenness, carousing, and things like these" (5:21). We live in a culture that is marked by substance abuse, whether it is alcohol, prescription drugs, illegal drugs, or narcotics. Things are so out of control in our society that people have now turned to abusing common household items like paint and aerosols.

The first substance oriented sin that Paul lists is "drunkenness." The Greek term *methe*, from which it is translated, was used to mean either strong drink or the result of strong drink which was drunkenness. Drunkenness is positioned throughout Scripture as the opposite to a life of obedience to God and faithful response to the Holy Spirit.

Tied to the first sin is the second, which is carousing, *komos* in the Greek. These two terms, *methe* and *komos*, were connected throughout the ancient world particularly in the context of the orgies and wild festivals associated with the worship of pagan gods. Since idolatry was mentioned earlier, the pagan festivals recede into the background and the focus is excessive revelry and merriment which results from drunkenness.

So Paul has given his list of sins that are produced by the flesh. These are things that the flesh desires to give rise to in a person's life. As we noted earlier, by the fact that Paul ends the list with "and things like these" indicates that the list is not meant to be exhaustive, but a sample. In the unsaved person these deeds are manifested without restraint. By that I do not mean that all of them are manifested in every unsaved person to the fullest degree, but rather those that are manifested reveal themselves as a natural, necessary, and expected consequence to who they are. In the saved person, however, these deeds manifest themselves only in a perverted and an abnormal way. These deeds are not a natural, necessary, and expected consequence of who they are, but rather are the remnants of a defeated flesh. Paul concludes with the consequences of these deeds.

## *The Consequences of Those Deeds*

Paul writes in the rest of 5:21, "of which I forewarn you just as I have forewarned you that those who practice such things shall not inherit the kingdom of God." Paul had at a previous time issued a warning to the Galatians that he refers to as a forewarning. To forewarn is to issue a notification of danger before the future event takes place to which the notification refers. Paul had given them notification regarding what this type of lifestyle produced. By the fact that he has to reissue the warning indicates that they are apparently still struggling with these issues. The warning itself is regarding "those who practice such things." The term for "practice" is one of two primary Greek words used to communicate action or the doing of something. The particular term the apostle uses here, *prasso*, focuses upon the doing of the action and not quite as much on the completion of the action being done. Its weight is on the carrying out part of the action. This form indicates that Paul's point is on habitual, ongoing, customary carrying out of these types of things. This is particularly important to understand in light of the KJV's translation of this phrase. In the KJV it reads, "they which do such things." The implication from that translation is, that if as a believer I do any of the things mentioned above even once, I am doomed to the warning that the apostle Paul makes here. The problem is, even after salvation, no person ever again refrains perfectly from committing sin. This is an unfortunate translation of these words. Paul's point in this text is the character or direction of your life. It is the person whose usual and habitual practice that is marked by the flesh that is not saved and therefore, as Paul says, not due "to inherit the kingdom of God." The believer's usual and habitual practice is righteousness, with temporary and sporadic failures to the flesh. Those individuals who claim Christ with their mouth and yet live unrestrained habitual lives of sin must be questioned as to the reality of their confession. The Galatians were no longer perpetually marked by such deeds, but needed to be warned nonetheless to retreat from the occasional doing of them. How were they to do that? By manifesting the Spirit's control, to which he now turned next.

# APPENDIX B

# The Fruit of the Spirit (Galatians 5:22-23)
# A Life Manifesting the Spirit's Control

Paul explained what the life devoid of the Spirit's control was like, so now in 5:22-23 he looks at the life of the branch which abides in Christ, bears fruit, and thus manifests the Spirit's control. In these two verses the reader learns of the unity of the Spirit's fruit, the fruit of the Spirit's working, and the consequence of that fruit.

## *The Unity of the Spirit's Fruit*

The unity of the Spirit's fruit is manifested in Paul's words "But the fruit of the Spirit is" (5:22a). You will note that "fruit," singular, stands in contrast to "deeds," plural. We should also note that "deeds" communicate the idea of products produced by a person's efforts. Fruit communicates, not products produced by a person's effort, but that which is a natural outgrowth. The point here is that the Spirit produces the following qualities in the believer's life as a set and as a natural result of His presence. To illustrate this point, one might refer to the apple which is a fruit and say that it is red, juicy, crunchy, sweet, and round. Now, by this we do not mean to refer to five different fruits, but rather one fruit with five different qualities. A healthy branch attached to a healthy vine will of necessity produce fruit. As fruit on a branch is a sure sign of a healthy branch, so fruit in the Christian's life is a sure sign of a healthy believer. Fruit is the outward attestation to the existence of internal salvation. Such presents to us and others the reality of our confession.

## *The Fruit of the Spirit's Working*

The aspects of the fruit of the Spirit that Paul lists here are nine, "love, joy, peace, patience, kindness, goodness, faithfulness, gentleness, self-control" (5:22b-23a). These nine aspects have not been effectively divided into groups, so we are going to look at them all under the general category of the fruit of the Spirit.

Paul begins with the prince of these aspects which is "love," agape. Paul has referred to agape love on two other occasions in this fifth chapter of Galatians already. In both references it was identified as the impetus of something else. In 5:6 it is the impetus to the believer's service of God, and in 5:13 it is the impetus to the believer's service of others. Love is to dominate all that the Christian does. In fact, Paul goes so far as to say in 1 Corinthians 13:1-3 that anything that the believer does, even to the point of giving up his life for someone else, is counted as nothing unless it is driven by agape. It was this love that drove Jesus to make the ultimate sacrifice of giving up His own life. Jesus Himself said in John 15:13, "Greater love has no one than this, that one lay down his life for his friends." But Christ's and God's love even exceeded this because Romans 5:8 says, "But God demonstrates His own love toward us, in that while we were yet sinners, Christ died for us." While people may die for friends, dying for enemies is completely out of the question. Yet such is what Christ did. Based on this pattern of love, Christ says in John 15:12, "This is My commandment, that you love one another, just as I have loved you." The believer is one who is willing to give up his life for his brothers.

While very few are asked to give the ultimate sacrifice of giving up their life, we cannot escape the attitude that would produce such, because Paul indicates that one of the manifestations of such a love is, according to Philippians 2:3-4, that we "do nothing from selfishness or empty conceit, but with humility of mind let each of you regard one another as more important than himself; do not *merely* look out for your own personal interests, but also for the interests of others."

The next aspect to the fruit of the Spirit is "joy." Joy, as with the case with each of these aspects of the fruit of the Spirit, is not possessed by Christians alone. Joy is a human emotion or feeling that is a reaction to pleasant circumstances or a life of peaceful balance. However, as with each of these aspects, the joy of the Christian is of a different origin and nature than that of the joy of mankind in general. First and foremost, joy is something that is possessed by God. The faithful servant is rewarded by being told to "enter into the joy of your master" (Mt. 25:21). This heavenly joy is particularly evidenced when sinners repent and turn to God (Lk. 15:7, 10, 32). Christian joy finds its origin in God. Being God Himself, Christ also possesses joy and is the ultimate origin of the believer's joy for He describes this reality in John 15:11 as follows, "These things I have spoken to you, that My joy may be in you, and that your joy may be made full" (Jn. 17:13). This joy is a gift and not earned for Romans 15:13 says, "May the God of hope fill you with all joy and peace in believing," and is a mark of God's kingdom according to Romans 14:17, "For the kingdom of God is not eating and drinking, but righteousness and peace and joy in the Holy Spirit."

      This joy is not only distinctive from human joy in its origin and how one comes to possess it, but it is also distinct in its character. First and foremost, Christians take joy in Christ. The angels told the shepherds, "Do not be afraid; for behold, I bring you good news of a great joy which shall be for all the people" (Luke 2:10). Christ is the epicenter of the believer's joy for 1 Peter 1:8 says, "and though you have not seen Him, you love Him, and though you do not see Him now, but believe in Him, you greatly rejoice with joy inexpressible and full of glory." Christians take joy in the ministry to other saints. Acts 15:3 says, "Therefore, being sent on their way by the church, they were passing through both Phoenicia and Samaria, describing in detail the conversion of the Gentiles, and were bringing great joy to all the brethren" (cf. 1 Thess. 3:9; 3 Jn. 4). But probably the most distinctive characteristic of Christian joy is its overcoming power.

## A LIFE MANIFESTING THE SPIRIT'S CONTROL

Unlike human joy, Christian joy is independent of circumstances. Human joy fluctuates with pleasant or harmonious circumstances, while Christian joy is on a wholly different plane than circumstances. For example, Paul writes, "I am overflowing with joy in all our affliction" (2 Cor. 7:4). In the midst of his suffering the apostle Paul writes to the Philippians, "But even if I am being poured out as a drink offering upon the sacrifice and service of your faith, I rejoice and share my joy with you all" (Phil.2:17), and in Colossians 1:24 he says, "Now I rejoice in my sufferings for your sake, and in my flesh I do my share on behalf of His body, which is the church, in filling up that which is lacking in Christ's afflictions." It was said of the Thessalonians in 1:6, "You also became imitators of us and of the Lord, having received the word in much tribulation with the joy of the Holy Spirit." James beckons all believers in 1:2, "Consider it all joy, my brethren, when you encounter various trials." In this reality, the believer imitates Christ because Hebrews 12:2 reads, "fixing our eyes on Jesus, the author and perfecter of faith, who for the joy set before Him endured the cross, despising the shame, and has sat down at the right hand of the throne of God."

So what is Christian joy? Christian joy is that divinely given disposition and state of being which delights in Christ and His benefits, being unencumbered by the positive or negative circumstances of this life, in which the Christian lives and abides. This is the joy that the Holy Spirit produces.

The Holy Spirit also produces peace. When Adam and Eve sinned in the Garden, the relationship between God and man changed. What at one time was an open, forthright relationship turned into one of hiddenness and concealment. The two parties who were at one time at peace with each other were now at war. Hostilities had broken out. The human side of this war is described as unsaved man being "hostile toward God" (Rom. 8:7; cf. Jam. 4:4). The divine side is described as the "wrath of God" (Rom. 1:18; 2:5-6; 3:3-6). Peace is that characteristic of God's relationship with His children that places the two parties at harmony with each other through the reconciliation effected by Jesus Christ. This peace manifests itself or produces the other aspects of peace that are part of the believer's life. This peace leads to peace of mind and heart that can only come from a relationship with Jesus Christ (cp. Phil. 4:7 and Jn. 14:27). This peace also leads to peace between various groups within the church due to the unity that God's peace has brought into existence (Eph. 2:11-22). This peace with God, which leads to the peace of God, is based on the reconciliation between God and man, of which the Christian is a spokesman (2 Cor. 5:18-21).

The next aspect to the fruit that the Spirit produces is patience. This comes from the Greek term *makrothumia*. This is not the patience we imagine in which one passively waits for something to take place or not to take place. It is a very active word. The idea is more endurance, long-suffering, or forbearance in spite of persecution or provocation which would normally produce otherwise. It is self-restraint which does not retaliate a wrong. Again, as with the previous aspects, this aspect finds its origin in God.

Paul described God in Romans 2:4 as being rich in "kindness and forbearance and patience" (c.f. Ex. 34:6). This is an evidence of God's grace because it is even extended to those condemned to hell for Romans 9:22 says, "What if God, although willing to demonstrate His wrath and to make His power known, endured with much patience vessels of wrath prepared for destruction?" His endurance with mankind is for the purpose of salvation for the chosen (1 Tim. 1:16; 2 Pet. 3:9, 15). God gives this quality to His children. It is a part of their calling. Believers are told to walk worthy of their calling in Ephesians 4:1, which means that they are to walk "with patience, showing forbearance to one another in love" (v. 2). Although given by God, believers are to pursue it, attempting to attain "all steadfastness and patience" (Col. 1:11; cf. 3:12). Patience for the believer is a divinely given and produced endurance of situations of hardship and forbearance of wrongs and injuries by others.

The fifth aspect to the fruit is "kindness," *chrestotes* in the Greek. Again, we are not surprised to see that kindness is a quality of the divine before it is ever a quality of the Christian. As noted earlier, kindness is claimed in both Romans 2:4 and Exodus 34:6 to be a quality of God. In fact, it is based upon His kindness that He saved us for Titus 3:4-5 says, "But when the kindness of God our Savior and His love for mankind appeared, He saved us." It is to mark all Christians and is specifically brought forward in reference to leaders of whom 2 Timothy 2:24 says, "And the Lord's bond-servant must not be quarrelsome, but be kind to all, able to teach, patient when wronged." Of this quality God makes the following statement in Micah 6:8, "He has told you, O man, what is good; And what does the Lord require of you but to do justice, to love kindness, and to walk humbly with your God?" We might define Christian kindness as divinely given and produced; a good-hearted and benevolent disposition that is concretely expressed toward one's neighbor for the glory of Christ.

The Spirit will also produce "goodness" in the life of the believer. This term, *agathosyne*, is related to two other New Testament terms. It is derived from the term *agathos*, which means good, and is related to *agathopoiia* which means to do good. The *agathos* is the morally correct person, who does good, which is *agathopoiia*. This person possesses a goodness, that is a good will or a kindly intention that seeks the best of and for others. This quality, also, is a characteristic of God (Psa. 23:6; 27:13). It is attached to the believer's calling and glorifies Christ when it is practiced, for Paul says that the goal of his prayer for the Thessalonians was "that our God may count you worthy of your calling, and fulfill every desire for goodness and the work of faith with power; in order that the name of our Lord Jesus may be glorified" (2 Thess. 1:11-12). Goodness is tied to being in the light (Eph. 5:9) and is part of a circumspect Christian lifestyle (Eph. 5:15-17). Notice Paul's words in Galatians 6:10, "So then, while we have opportunity, let us do good to all men, and especially to those who are of the household of the faith."

Next in the list is "faithfulness." This is derived from the common New Testament term *pistis*. The faithfulness of God is indeed great, as Lamentations 3:23 says, and is manifested in the consistency of His lovingkindness and compassion. It is upon this that the believer can take courage and hope because Paul writes, "Faithful is He who calls you, and He also will bring it to pass" (1 Thess. 5:24). Faithfulness is also a quality of Christ, who faithfully performed the Father's will to the completed end, so that He is described as the one who is Faithful and True (Rev. 19:11). This divine quality is manifested in God's children through the Spirit. Faithfulness is the ultimate barometer or scale that indicates whether Christians have been effective in their stewardship of life. Matthew 25:21 records a parabolic illustration of Christ's evaluation of the believer and records, "His master said to him, 'Well done, good and faithful slave; you were faithful with a few things, I will put you in charge of many things.'" It is so much a part of them that we are described in the Revelation as those who are "called and chosen and faithful" (Rev. 17:14).

We are to also be marked by "gentleness," or *prautes* in the Greek. Unlike the other attributes or the fruit of the Spirit, this one is not identified as being possessed by God and is only attributed to Jesus Christ in His incarnation. Jesus says of Himself in Matthew 11:29, "for I am gentle and humble in heart." It is in imitation of the Savior that the Holy Spirit produces this disposition in the life of the believer. Although produced by the Spirit, it is to be walked in by the believer as a reflection of his calling and for the purpose of maintaining unity (Eph. 4:1-3; Col. 3:12-14). Gentleness refers to two specific qualities: that of a humble, submissive, and teachable spirit (Jam. 1:21) and a considerate and charitable approach to others (2 Tim. 2:25; 1 Pet. 3:15). Christian gentleness is a sign of great strength for it resists the natural pull of our humanity to exert ourselves over others, to payback evil for evil, to force our will on others, to hoard for ourselves, to assume the worse, to condemn with no understanding, and to treat people inhumanely. As one author rightly put it, "This receptivity toward one's neighbor, this affability, this kindness in relations" is gentleness. This was how Christ lived and how we are called to live as well.

Paul concludes his list with the ninth aspect of the fruit of the Spirit and that is self-control, *egkrateia*. Obviously, this attribute does not apply to God. As one pastor put it, "Perfect holiness possesses perfect control." Jesus, in His incarnation evidenced self-control, particularly as the devil assailed Him in temptation (Mt. 4:1-11). This term finds its origin in a Greek word that stood for control or mastery. Its meaning, when applied to self, was control or master of one's self particularly in reference to one's passions and appetites. Socrates and Aristotle made it in their ethical systems the very foundation of all other virtues and virtuous living. However, for the believer, self-control is very different than in their systems. In fact, it is almost an anomaly. After all, it is control of self and is given by another. It is a crucial aspect of our life as believers, so much so that Paul's presentation of Christianity to Felix, a Roman governor, included it as one of the three items, "And as he was discussing righteousness, self-control and the judgment to come, Felix became frightened" (Acts 24:25).

## *The Consequence of That Fruit*

These nine items are evident in all Christians' lives. In some believers the fruit is barely intelligible, but if they are truly Christ's, it is there. According to John 15 every Christian bears fruit, all are to bear more fruit, and it is God's will that they bear much fruit (v. 2, 4-5, 8). But these are not the only qualities, because Paul says, "against such things there is no law" (5:23b). There are other qualities such as hope, mercy, diligence, perseverance, purity, godliness, etcetera. However, this list gives us an idea of what our focus is to be upon. Paul's words here are somewhat sarcastic. Paul is saying, "Since these things are produced by the Spirit through faith and not by the Law that the Galatians are wanting to follow, does that mean that the Law of God prohibits these qualities? Are these the types of things that are ruled against in the Law?" Of course not. Such would be ludicrous. Rather, these are the very qualities that God wants manifested in believers' lives. They are not manifested by the Law, but by the Spirit.

## *Paul's Conclusion*

Paul concludes his presentation of the manifestation of the Spirit controlled life with a statement as to the ramifications of such a life. Having clearly explained what the life looks like, Paul now returns to the issue of how believers are to bring these things to the forefront of their lives. He has already alluded to the method by instructing them to walk by the Spirit and be led by the Spirit. In the last three verses he explains more fully this process.

## Personal Ramifications

Paul begins with the personal ramifications. What must they do personally? Paul instructs them to do two things, which are to mortify and vivify. Mortify means to put to death and vivify means to bring to life.

### *Mortify the Flesh*

The instructions regarding mortification are given in 5:24. Paul reminds them, "Now those who belong to Christ Jesus have crucified the flesh with its passions and desires." First, he identifies those to whom his statements apply as "those who belong to Christ." Being a part of Christ's body is only accomplished through what Paul identifies as crucifying the flesh. By its tense, Paul identifies this as a past action that has already taken place. Paul identified the fact that he had experienced a crucifixion in Galatians 2:20. This crucifixion is the one that all believers experience and which is identified in Romans 6:1-7. This crucifixion put to death our old man, freeing us from the irresistible tyranny of sin, because he was replaced with a new man. However, sin is still at work in the reality of the Christian's life, due to us still having a sinful body with sin's principle still active in it (Rom. 7:17-23). This ongoing sin problem is why Paul indicates through the tense of the verb "have crucified" that this past event has ongoing ramifications. The idea here is that what God did in mortifying our old man, that is our constitutional flesh, believers are to imitate by continuing to mortify the sin principle in the physical flesh, that is our systemic flesh. Unless we continuously kill the desires and passions of the flesh, we will have no hope of avoiding its deeds. To kill the desires and passions of the flesh: 1) starve them (Rom. 13:14); 2) flee from them (1 Cor. 6:18); 3) recognize the danger of internalized sin (Mt. 5:21-30; Mk. 7:20-23); 4) understand the anatomy of a sin and guard yourself from your own sinful tendencies (1 Thess. 4:4; Jam. 1:14-15); and 5) by all means, pray for victory (1 Thess. 5:17; 1 Jn. 5:14-15).

*Vivify the Spirit*

One will not be victorious by just killing the deeds of the body, but he must also liven what God has placed into him at salvation. It was Paul who said to work out what God worked in (Phil. 2:12-13). That principle is stated this way in Galatians 5:25, "If we live by the Spirit, let us also walk by the Spirit." One's possession of the Spirit demands a certain "walk." This is a different term than what appears in 5:16. Here Paul uses the Greek word *stoicheo*, which referred to soldiers who marched in battle-order. It meant to keep in line with or keep in step with another or a particular standard. The claim of being a Christian can only be humanly validated by a life that reflects the presence of the Spirit, that is, the Spirit's fruit. He must keep up with what the Spirit is producing, he must work out what God has worked in. How do you keep in step with the Spirit? Well Jesus said that the Spirit came to "guide the disciples into all the truth" (John 16:13), and He indicated that God's "word is truth" (John 17:17). You keep in step with the Spirit and are led by the Spirit by keeping in step with the Word of God, which demands hearing the word taught, studying the word for yourself, and obeying what the word says.

    Paul has indicated in these two verses that the Spirit controlled life means that you respond to God's killing of your old man by killing the residue of his effects which still remain in your flesh, and that you respond to the Spirit's creation of His fruit in your life by cultivating that fruit's growth.

# Endnotes

1. Oded Borowski, *Agriculture in Iron Age Israel* (Winona Lake: Eisenbrauns, 1987), 106.

2. Ibid, 105.

3. David C. Hopkins argues along very similar lines in *The Highlands of Canaan: Agricultural Life in the Early Iron Age*, vol. 3, *The Social World of Biblical Antiquity Series* (Decatur: The Almond Press, 1985), 228.

4. Borowski, 108-109.

5. Ibid, 108.

6. Ibid, 107-108.

7. Ibid., 109; Hopkins, 228.

8. James B. Pritchard, *The Ancient Near East*, (Princeton: Princeton University Press, 1958), fig. 19.

9. Ibid.

10. Borowski, 111-112.

11. Ibid, 110, 112.

12. Ibid., 112; Ralph Gower, *The New Manners and Customs of Bible Times*, (Chicago: Moody Press, 1987), 109.

13. Ibid, 109.

14. Ibid., 112; Gower, 109.

15. Hopkins, 229.

16. John MacArthur, *The MacArthur Bible Commentary*, (Nashville: Thomas Nelson, 2005), 857.

www.ingramcontent.com/pod-product-compliance
Lightning Source LLC
Chambersburg PA
CBHW020933090426
42736CB00010B/1119